RAMTHA

An Introduction

edited by

Steven Lee Weinberg, Ph.D.

D0047847

Sovereignty, Inc.

BF
1301
.R2344
1988

To Ernest Kanzler
for his love of the teachings
and his generous support of Sovereignty

RAMTHA:
AN INTRODUCTION

Copyright © 1988 by Sovereignty, Inc.

All rights reserved. Printed in the United States of America. No part of this book may be reproduced without prior written consent of the publisher, except brief quotes used in newspaper or magazine reviews. This work is derived in part from Ramtha Dialogues®, magnetic tape recordings authored by JZ Knight, with her permission. Ramtha Dialogues® is a trademark registered with the U.S. Patent Trademark Office.

DISCLAIMER

This book is designed to provide information in regard to the subject matter covered. The purpose of this book is to educate and entertain. The author, editors, and publisher shall have neither liability nor responsibility to any person or entity with respect to any loss or damage caused, or alleged to be caused, directly or indirectly, by the information contained in this book.

ISBN 0932201-76-8
Library of Congress Catalog Card Number: 87-60651

Book and Cover Design/Carol Wright

ACKNOWLEDGEMENTS

We thank Sara Steinberg, Carol Wright, and John Clancy for their editorial assistance, and Richard Cohn for permission to use photographs of Ramtha, from the book *I Am Ramtha,* © 1987 Beyond Words Publisher.

FOR MORE INFORMATION

For information about audiences with Ramtha, books, and audio and video cassettes presenting Ramtha's teachings, please see the back of this book.

Third Printing/April 1989

Sovereignty, Inc.
Box 926, Eastsound, WA 98245

Foreword

Since 1981, I have been examining, experiencing, and rejoicing in the wisdom of Ramtha—a deeply loving, eloquent, and outrageous intelligence who has been channeling his teachings through the body of JZ Knight. My process of critically examining the teacher and his message has involved listening to and transcribing more than 2000 hours of tape-recorded public and private audiences presented by Ramtha since 1978.

Out of my desire to share Ramtha's teachings with others— and to organize them for my own understanding—I edited RAMTHA, the critically acclaimed "white book" that presents the foundations of the teachings. Published in 1986, this book is considered by many to be one of the most significant presentations of "new age" thought.

Because of the growing interest in Ramtha's teachings, I saw the need for a book which would allow a wider audience to get a feel for who Ramtha is and what he teaches, yet one which would also be of great value for those who have already read RAMTHA.

Ramtha: An Introduction was prepared to accomplish both objectives. It is an informative, easy-to-read, and entertaining collection of edited transcripts that have been selected to provide a rich sampling of Ramtha's wisdom on a diversity of topics.

I am very pleased to be able to share this work with you. I know you will find it an extremely powerful and enjoyable

CONCORDIA COLLEGE LIBRARY
2811 NE HOLMAN ST.
PORTLAND, OR 97211-6099

reading experience. For many, it will profoundly affect your perspective of life and set in motion a process of change that will take you, as it is taking me, into a freedom and joy that only tears can express.

Contents

*"You were born a knowing god,
yet you were brought up
to have it reasoned out of you.*

*I will teach you
how to be
like a little child again."*

For The Love
Of Your Being

I am Ramtha, a sovereign entity who lived a long time ago upon this plane called Earth, or Terra. In that life, I did not die; I ascended, for I learned to harness the power of thought and to take my body with me into an unseen dimension of life. In doing so, I realized an existence of unlimited freedom, unlimited joy, unlimited life. Others who lived on Terra after my time have also ascended.

I am now part of an unseen brotherhood who love mankind, greatly. We are your brothers who hear your prayers and your meditations and observe your movements to and fro. We are those who lived here as man and experienced the despair, the sorrow, and the joy that all of you have known. Yet we learned to master and transcend the human experience to realize a grander state of being.

I have come to tell you that you are very important and precious to us, because the life that flows through you and the thought that is coming to every one of you—however you entertain it—is the intelligence and life-force that you have termed God. It is this essence that connects us, not only with those upon your plane, but with those in untold universes that you have not now the eyes to see.

This chapter has been excerpted and edited from *RAMTHA*, Sovereignty, Inc., 1986.

I am here to remind you of a heritage you forgot long, long ago. I have come to give you a loftier perspective from which you may reason and understand that you are, indeed, divine and immortal entities who have always been loved and supported by the essence called God. I am here to help you realize that you alone, through your divine intelligence and freedom of will, have created every reality in your life; and with that same power, you have the option to create and experience *any* reality you desire.

For ages you have been taught that God is outside your kingdom, somewhere in the depths of space. Many of you have believed this and accepted it as a truth. But God, the principal cause of all life, has never been *outside* of you; it *is* you. It is the unlimited thought process, the supreme intelligence that lies forgotten but ever-present within man.

You have been taught that you are born only to live in a moment of time, to grow old, and then die. Because you have believed that to be true, it has *indeed* become the reality upon this plane. But I am here to help you realize that you are forever entities who have been living *billions* of years—ever since God, your beloved Father, the totality of Thought, contemplated itself into the brilliance of Light, a particum of which each of you became. That is when each of you came to be unique and sovereign and a forever part of the intelligence called the Mind of God.

You have been taught that God is a singular entity who with his hands made heaven and earth, and then created the living creature called man. But it is *you* who are the great creators of *all life*. It is you who created the morning sun, the evening sky, and the loveliness of everything that is. It is you who created the remarkable creature called man, so that you, who were brilliant lights in the void of space, could experience the wonderment of your created forms.

My beloved brothers, your understanding of who you are is a collection of illusions you have been living for *millions* of years. Who are you? You are far, far greater than the limited creature called man. •You are God. You are gods created of God, sons created of the Father—the first and only direct creation of the source of all life. In your adventures into the exploration of Life, each of you has integrated your sublime intelligence with cellular matter to become *god-man*: a part of the Mind of God expressing in the form called humanity; a god living in the wonderment of his own creation, termed man. Mankind, womankind, humanity—you are God, indeed, wonderfully disguised as limited, wretched entities.

Most of you have been returning to this place called Earth, life after life after life, for the ten million years that man has lived here as God incarnate. Why? Because you became so immersed in the illusions of this plane that you forgot the *awesome* power that flows through you. And in ten million years, you have gone from being sovereign and all-powerful entities, to where you are now—utterly lost in matter; enslaved by your own creations of dogma, law, fashion and tradition; separated by country, creed, sex and race; immersed in jealousy, bitterness, guilt and fear. Through groveling for survival, you forgot the greatness that you are.

Many teachers have come to you throughout your history, and we have tried many different avenues to remind you of who you are. We have been king, conqueror, slave, hero, crucified Christ, teacher, guide, friend, philosopher—whatever would bring *knowledge* to this plane. At times we have intervened in your affairs to keep you from annihilating yourselves, so that life here would continue to provide a playground for your experiences and your evolution into joy. But one by one you persecuted those who reached out to help you. Those you didn't persecute, you made statues of, and you twisted and perverted their words for your own designs. Instead of applying their teachings, you ended up worshiping the teachers.

To prevent you from worshiping me, I have not come to you in my own embodiment. Instead, I have chosen to speak to you through an entity who was my beloved daughter when I

lived upon this plane. My daughter, who graciously allows me
to use her embodiment, is a pure channel for the essence that I
am. When I speak to you, she is no longer within her body,
for her soul and spirit have left it completely.

I am indeed your *equal*, for no one in the kingdom of God,
seen or unseen, can ever be greater or less than you. I am not a
messiah, a savior, or a deliverer. And I am not the stairway to
what you term heaven. I will show you where it is, but it is up
to you to embrace the wisdom that will take you there.

Am I a reality? Well, are *you*? Who are you that hides within the embodiment that *you* are using? What is the unseen essence that makes your body work, that smiles at the laughter
of children, that rejoices at the wonderment of a sunrise, that
dreams tomorrow into reality? If I were to remove your body,
no one could see that which you be, yet you would still be
there. Your body is only an illusionary vehicle for you to ride
within, so that the unseen personality that you are may experience the plane of three-dimensional matter.

I realize it will be difficult for you to accept the reality I am,
but you have yet to listen through any other means. So I will
teach you as an unseen enigma, just as you yourself are behind
the mask that you wear. And you will learn, greatly, but from
an entity who has no body for you to hold on to, no temple for
you to worship in, and no image to which you can pray. The
grandest temple is your own body. The most exquisite and
beautiful garden lies within your own soul. And you, who
have the power to create eternity, you are your *own* savior.

I have not come here to *tell* you of the splendor that lies beyond this place, but to help you see it for yourself—and not
through *philosophical* understandings, but through teachings
that ring so blatantly true within you, that your soul *urges* you
to become the divine principle you forgot long ago. And for
you to continue as a race of entities in this form, it is most important that you learn of your own divinity, as well as everyone else's.

Through the power of my being and for the love of your being, I will teach you, as I taught myself, how to return to your greatness. And in your joy, I will laugh with you; when you weep, I will send a wind to dry your tears.

Through this teaching, you will learn to be the sovereign god that you were in all your glory when you began your re-markable journey. You will learn to listen solely to the voice within you and to follow only the path of joy. You will learn how to feel, profoundly, so you gain the truest treasure of this plane: emotion. And you will come to love yourself so grand-ly that no matter *who* stands before you, you will find God in them, and you will love them as deeply as you have learned to love yourself. Then you, who have taught yourself so elo-quently, will be a brilliant light to the world—only because you are a radiant example of the love of self.

Now, this teaching is *not* a religious understanding, for reli-gion is dogmatic, restrictive, and very judgmental. This teach-ing is simply *knowledge*. It is learning, it is experience, it is love. I will *love* you into knowing God and being the unlimit-edness that God is.

This teaching possesses *no laws*, for law is a limitation that obstructs freedom. I will teach you of nothing but God and op-tions. I am here to open the doors to greater knowledge so you realize your options for living upon this plane; so you realize that your life is not limited to this plane, for life exists in many other places.

I am here to help you, who are enslaved by fear and en-trapped by your own thought processes, to begin to see a new vista of unlimited thinking, unlimited purpose, unlimited life. I ask of you nothing other than to be yourself. But most here do not know *who* self is. I will teach you how to find it once more. And when found, you will *never* let go of it again. Then you will need no one to teach you thereafter. Then you are sovereign in your own truth and free to live according to your own designs.

Now, I have brought with me the winds of change upon your plane. I join those who stand with me in preparing mankind for a grand event that has already been set into motion. We are going to unite all the people of this plane by allowing man to witness something great and brilliant, which will cause him to open up and allow knowledge and love to flow forth.

Why is this being done? Because you are loved, greater than you have ever thought possible. And because it is time for man to live a grander understanding than that which has plagued him into dark ages, taken away his freedom, divided peoples, and caused hatred between lovers and war amongst nations.

There is coming a day, very soon, when great knowledge will be brought to this plane by entities who are your beloved brothers. In that time, scientific developments will bloom here greater than they ever have.

What is coming forth is called the *Age of God*. This age will come about, in part, through a deliberate change in the value of time. In the years to come, disease, suffering, hatred, and war will no longer be upon this plane. No longer will there be the aging and death of the body, but continuous life. It is through knowledge, understanding, and profound love that these things will come forth in the life of each entity.

There is no other redemption for mankind than to realize their divinity. You are the seeds of this understanding. As each of you realizes your own value and the foreverness of your life, you will add to the consciousness of unlimited thinking, unlimited freedom, unlimited love. For whenever you realize a grander understanding, you lift and expand consciousness *everywhere*. And when you *live* what you have come to understand, wholly for the good of your own purposeful life, you allow others to see in you a greater thought process, a grander understanding, a more purposeful and joyful existence than what they see all around them.

These are the greatest of all times in your recorded history. Though they are difficult and challenging times, you chose to experience them for the fulfillment they would bring you. All of you have been promised for e'er so long that you would see God in your lifetime. Yet lifetime after lifetime you never allowed yourselves to see it. In this lifetime, most of you will indeed. You will live to see a magnificent kingdom emerge here, and civilizations will come forth that you had not even the slightest notion existed. And a new wind will blow. And love, peace, and joy in being will grace this blessed place, the emerald of your universe and the home of God.

Contemplate what has been spoken. Allow these words within your being. When you do, thought by thought, feeling by feeling, moment by moment, you will come back into the understanding of your greatness, your power, and your glory.

***

2

I Am Ramtha

I am Ramtha, "the Ram." In the ancient language of my times, it means "the god." I am the great Ram of the Hindu people, for I was the first man born of the womb of woman and the loins of man who ever ascended from this plane. I learned how to ascend, not through the teachings of any man, but through the profound realization that God lives in everything. I was also a man who hated and despised, who slew and conquered and ruled—right into my enlightenment.

I was the first conqueror this plane knew. I began a march that lasted 63 years, and I conquered three-quarters of the known world. But my greatest conquest was of myself. When I learned to love myself and embrace the whole of life, I ascended with the wind into forever.

I ascended in front of my people on the northeast side of the mount called Indus. My people, who numbered more than two million, were a mixture of Lemurians, people from Ionia, and tribespeople escaping from Atlatia, the land you call Atlantis. My people's lineage now makes up the populace of India, Tibet, Nepal, and southern Mongolia.

I lived but one lifetime upon this plane, what is called in your understanding of time, 35,000 years ago. I was born to an unfortunate people, pilgrims from the land called Lemuria living in the slums of Onai, the greatest port city of Atlatia in its

Excerpted and edited from *RAMTHA*.

southern sphere.

I came to Atlatia during what is called "the last hundred years," before great waters covered its land. At that time, Atlatia was a civilization of people with great intellect, whose endowment for scientific understanding was superb. Their science was even greater than what you have at this time, for the Atlatians had begun to understand and use the principles of light. They knew how to transform light into pure energy. They even had primitive aeroships that traveled on light, a science provided to them through an intercommunication with entities from other star systems. Because of the Atlatians' great involvement with technology, they worshiped the intellect, and it became their religion.

The Lemurians were quite different from the Atlatians. Their social system was built upon communication through thought. They had not the advancement of technology, only a great spiritual understanding, for my forefathers were grand in their knowingness of unseen values. They revered that which was beyond the moon, beyond the stars. They *loved* an essence that could not be identified, a power they called the *Unknown God*. Because the Lemurians worshiped only this God, the Atlatians despised them, for they despised anything that was not "progressive."

When I was a little boy, life was destitute and very arduous. At that particular point in time, Atlatia had lost its technology, for its scientific centers in the north had been destroyed long ago. In their experiments with traveling on light, the Atlatians had pierced the cloud cover that completely surrounded your planet, much as it surrounds Venus today. When they pierced the cloud cover, great waters fell and a freeze occurred, which put most of Lemuria and the northern part of Atlatia under deep oceans. Thus the people from Lemuria and the north of Atlatia fled to the southern regions of Atlatia.

Once technology was lost in the north, life gradually became primitive in the south. During the hundred years before all of Atlatia was submerged, the southernmost region had degenerated into the rule of tyrants who governed the people through irrefutable law. Under the abominable rule of these tyrants, the Lemurians were considered the dung of the earth, less than a dog in the street.

Contemplate for a moment being spat upon, urinated upon, and allowed to wash it away only with your tears. Contemplate knowing that the dogs in the streets have greater nourishment than you, who hunger for anything to kill the agony in your belly.

In the streets of Onai, it was common to see the brutalization of children and the beating and rape of women. It was common to see Atlatians pass a starving Lemurian on the road and hold their noses with kerchiefs of fine linen, dipped in jasmine and rose water, for we were considered stinking, wretched things. We were "no-things, soulless, mindless wastes of intellect" because we were without the scientific understanding of such things as gases and light. Because we did not possess an intellectual bent, as it were, we were turned into slaves to work the fields.

Into such a life I was born upon this plane. That was my time. What sort of dream was I in? The beginning of man's advent into the arrogance and stupidity of intellect.

I did not blame my mother that I did not know who my father was. I did not blame my brother that our fathers were not the same. Nor did I blame my mother for our absolute poverty.

As a little boy, I watched as my mother was taken into the streets and had her sweetness taken from her. After my mother was taken, I watched a child grow inside her belly. And I watched my mother weep, for would there be another child to suffer as we had suffered in this "promised land"?

Because my mother was too weak to bear the child alone, I helped her give birth to my little sister. I scrounged in the streets for food, killed dogs and wildfowl, and stole grain from proprietors late in the evening, for I was very deft on my feet. I fed my mother, who in turn suckled my little sister.

I did not blame my little sister for the death of my beloved mother, for the little girl suckled away all of my mother's strength. My sister became diarrhetic and could not hold what was going into her body; and so she too lost all the life in her body.

I gathered together some timbers and laid my mother and sister on top of them. Then I stole away into the night to gather fire. I said a prayer to my mother and my sister, whom I loved greatly. Then I lit the timbers swiftly so that the stench from their bodies would not disturb the Atlatians, for if it did, the Atlatians would fling their bodies into the desert where the hyenas would tear them apart.

As I watched my mother and sister burn, my hatred for the Atlatians increased within my being to where it became like venom from a great viper—and I was only a little boy!

As the stench and smoke from the fire spread throughout the valley, I thought about the Unknown God of my people. I could not understand the injustice of this great God, or why he would create the monsters who hated my people so. What did my mother and little sister ever do to deserve the wretched deaths they experienced?

I did not blame the Unknown God for not loving me. I did not blame him for not loving my people. I did not blame him for the deaths of my mother and my sister. I did not blame him—I *hated* him!

I had no one left, for my brother had been kidnapped by a satrap and taken into subserviency to the land that would later be called Persia. There he would be abused for the pleasure of the satrap and his need for what is called loin gratification.

I was a lad of 14 with no meat upon my bones but a great bitterness inside me. So I decided to do battle with the Unknown God of my forefathers, the only thing I felt worthy of dying by. I was determined to die, but as an honorable man, and I felt that dying at the hands of man was a dishonorable way to perish.

I saw a great and mysterious mountain that loomed on the distant horizon. I thought if there were a God, he would live there, above us all, just as those who governed our land lived above us. If I could climb there, I thought, I would get in touch with the Unknown God and proclaim my hatred for him at his unfairness to my people.

I left my hovel and journeyed for many days to reach this great mountain, devouring locusts, ants, and roots along the way. When I reached the mount, I climbed into the clouds, which now veiled its whitened peak. I called out to the Unknown God, "I am a man! Why have I not the dignity of one?" And I demanded that he show me his face . . . but he ignored me.

I fell upon my haunches and wept heartily, until the whiteness iced itself from my tears. When I looked up, I beheld before me what seemed to be a wondrous woman holding a great sword. She spoke to me saying, "O Ram, you who are broken in spirit, your prayers have been heard. Take this sword and conquer yourself." And in but a blink of my eye she was gone.

Conquer myself? I could not turn the blade around and hack off my own head—my arms could not reach the hilt of the sword! Yet I found honor in this great sword. No longer did I shiver against the great cold but found warmth instead. And when I looked again where my tears had fallen, there grew a flower of such sweet aroma and color that I knew it was a bloom of hope.

I came down from the mountain with the great sword in my hand, a day recorded in the history of the Hindu people as *The Terrible Day of the Ram*. A boy had gone to that mountain, but a man returned. No longer frail in body, I was a Ram in every sense of the word. I was a young man with a terrible light about me and a sword larger than I was. Sometimes I think I was very slow to understand in that existence, for I never really questioned how the wondrous sword could be so light that I could carry it, yet so large that nine hands together could hold the hilt of it.

I returned from the mountain to the city of Onai. In the fields outside the city I saw an old woman stand up and shade her eyes to look at me a-coming. Soon, all stopped their labors. Carts stopped. Donkeys squealed. Then everything became quiet. When the people looked upon my countenance, they must have been deeply moved, because each immediately took up his meager tool and followed me into the city.

We destroyed Onai because the Atlatians spat in my eye when I demanded they open the granaries to feed our people. And they were easily overtaken, for they did not know of battle.

I opened the granaries to our poor people, then we slew the Atlatians and burned Onai to the ground. I never considered whether I could do that, for I did not care at that point if I lived or died; I had nothing left to live for.

When the slaughter and burning were finished, a great hurt was still within my being, for my hatred had not been satisfied. So I ran from the people to hide in the hills, but they followed me—in spite of all my cursing, throwing stones, and spitting at them.

"Ram, Ram, Ram, Ram," they chanted, carrying their tools of the field and grain tied in linens, and herding sheep and goats before them. I shouted at the people to leave me alone and go home, but still they came—for they no longer had a home! *I* was their home!

Since they insisted on following wherever I went, I gathered together all these "soulless" creatures of different denominations, and they became my army, my people. And great people were they indeed. But soldiers? Hardly. Nonetheless, that was when the great army of the Ram assembled itself. Its number in the beginning was close to ten thousand.

From that time, I was driven to slay tyranny and to make the color of my skin more respectable. And from all the sieges and battles we put forth, the lands we crossed, and all the people we freed along the way, greatly did my people grow . . . and great became the legend of the Ram and his army.

For the next 10 years, I was a driven entity, a barbarian who despised the tyranny of men. And I fought fully expecting to die. I did not have the fear of dying that many of my people did—because I *wanted* to die, honorably. So I never knew fear, I knew only hate.

When you lead a charge and you're the one in front, with no one on either side of you, you have to be crazed, filled with the powerful emotion called hate. So I was very much a spectacle to be hewn down by my foes (if they would only do me the honor). And I picked the worthiest opponents to be my demise. But you know, when there is an absence of fear, there is a presence of conquering. Thus, I became a great conqueror. Before my time there was no such thing as a conqueror, only tyrants.

I *created* war. I was the first conqueror this plane ever knew. Through my anger and my desire to be noble and to honor what I felt, I became what you would term a great entity. Know you what a hero is? Well, I was one indeed. The hero salvages life and puts an end to the wrongs of life, not realizing that in doing so, he is also creating a wrong. I desired to do battle with all forms of tyranny. And I did—only to become the very thing I despised.

I was an ignorant entity, an imbecile, a buffoon. And for 10 years into my march, I warred upon innocents and hacked and burned my way across many lands—until I was run through with a great sword. Had they left it in me, I might have been all right, but they pulled it out to make sure I would bleed to death.

I fell face downward onto the floor. As I lay on the snowy marbled floor—that seemingly was perfect—I saw that the river of scarlet had found a crack in it.

As I lay there, watching life ebbing from my being, I heard

a voice. It spoke to me, and it said, "Stand up." It repeated, "Stand up!"

I lifted up my head and put forth my palms. Then I began to draw under me the knees of my being. As I raised my body so that my head was erect and even, I pulled up my left foot and stabilized it. Then, gathering all of my strength, I put my hand upon my knee, my fist into my wound . . . and I stood up.

As I stood there, with blood issuing from my mouth, flowing from my wound, and running down my legs, my assailants, who were now certain that I was immortal, fled from me. My soldiers laid siege to the city and burned it to the ground.

I would never forget the voice that made me stand up, that kept me from dying. In the years to come I would search for the face of that voice.

I was given to the court of women in my march to be cared for. And it was, indeed, a most humiliating experience, for I was bossed by the women and undressed before their eyes. I could not even urinate or spill dung from my anus in private, but had to do it in front of them. And I had to endure the stinking poultices of vulture grease that were put upon my chest (I am convinced that the vulture grease was used not because it could heal me, but because it was so wretched to breathe that it kept life in me).

During my healing, much of my pride and hate had to give way to survival.

While I was recovering from my ghastly wound and couldn't do anything else, I began to contemplate everything around me. One day I watched an old woman pass from this plane, clutching the crudely woven linen she had made for her son, who had perished long ago. As I watched the old woman begin to shrivel in the light of the noonday sun, her mouth opened to an aghast expression and her eyes became glazed, unaffected by the light. Nothing moved save the breeze and her old hair.

I thought about the great intelligence of the woman and her

son, who had now both perished. Then I looked back at the sun, which never perished. It was the very same sun the old woman had seen through a crack in the roof of her hovel when she first opened her eyes as a babe . . . and it was the last thing she saw when she died.

I looked again at the sun. You know, it was oblivious that she had died. And I watched it as my men buried the old woman under a tall poplar tree by the river.

As the sun set that evening, I cursed it. I watched it sit upon the mantle of the mountains like a great fiery jewel. I looked upon the purpled mountains and the valley, already shrouded in mist, and saw rods of the sun's light gild all things and make them illusionarily beautiful. I saw clouds, once the color of blue, become vividly alive in hues of scarlet, fire-rose, and pink.

I watched the great light as it retired behind the mountains, now looming on the horizon like piercing teeth. Just as the last rods of the sun's beauty gave way to the advancing night, I heard a night bird cry above me, and I looked into the heavens to see a pale moon rising against a darkening sky. A breeze came up, and it blew my hair and dried my tears, and I felt a terrible sickness in my being.

You know, I was a great warrior. With a sword I could cleave a man in half in a moment. I had beheaded, hacked, and butchered. I had smelled blood and burned people. But why did I do all of that? The sun set in its magnificence anyway. The bird cried in the night, anyway. And the moon came up in spite of it all.

That is when I began to ponder the Unknown God. The only thing I truly wanted, was to understand this unseen essence that seemed so awesome, so mysterious, so very far away from man. And what was *man*? Why was he not greater than the sun? Why was man—the teeming multitude upon the plane, the creating force—seemingly the most vulnerable of all creations? If man was as important as my people acclaimed, why wasn't he important enough that when he died, the sun stood still to mourn his passing? Or the moon turned purple? Or the fowl ceased to fly? Man seemed very unimportant, for everything continued on in spite of his peril.

All I wanted was to know.

I did not have a teacher to teach me of the Unknown God, for I did not trust any man. I had seen and lost so much through the wickedness of man. I had seen men despise other men and think them to be soulless. I had seen innocents gutted and burned out of fear. I had seen children, naked on slave blocks, examined by perverted souls who plucked from the children their hairs of adolescence so they would still have the image of young children as they were raped. I had seen priests and prophets invent, through their hatred for mankind, creatures of great torment and ugliness, so they could govern and enslave people through the rule of religious forms.

No man living would I have as my teacher, for any man living had altered thinking—had taken that which was pure and innocent, and altered it through his own limited understanding. So I wanted nothing to do with a god created through man's understanding, for if man created the god, the god was fallible.

• It was life's elements that taught me of the Unknown God. I learned from days. I learned from nights. I learned from tender, insignificant life that abounded even in the face of destruction and war.

I contemplated the sun in its advent of glory upon the horizon. I watched its journey through the heavens, ending up in the western sphere and passing into its sleep. I learned that the sun, though mute, subtly controlled life; for all who were warring with one another, ceased their warring when the sun went down.

I watched the beauty of the moon in her pale light as she danced across the heavens, illuminating the darkness in mysterious and wonderful ways. I saw how the fires from our encampment lit up the evening sky. I listened to wildfowl land-ing on the water, birds rustling in their night nest, and children in their laughter. I observed falling stars, nightingales, the frost on the reeds, and the lake silvered with ice to create the illusion of another world. I observed women standing in the river as they gathered water in their urns, their clothing tied up in knots to reveal their alabaster knees. I listened to the clatter of their gossip and the teasing in their laughter. I smelled the smoke from distant fires and the garlic and wine on the breath of my men.

It was not until I observed and pondered life and its ongoingness, that I discovered who the Unknown God truly was. I reasoned that the Unknown God was not the gods created through the altered thinking of man. I realized that the gods in men's minds are only the personalities of the things they fear and respect the most; that the true God is the ongoing essence that permits man to create and play out his illusions however he chooses, and that will still be there when man returns yet again, another spring, another life. I realized that it is in the power and the ongoingness of the Life Force where the Unknown God truly lies.

Who was the Unknown God? It was me . . . and the birds in their night nest, the frost on the reeds, the morning dawn and evening sky. It was the sun and the moon, children and their laughter, alabaster knees and running water, and the smell of garlic and leather and brass. This understanding took a long time for me to grasp, though it had been right in front of me all along. The Unknown God wasn't *beyond* the moon or the sun—it was all *around* me!

With this new birth of reasoning I began to embrace life, to hold life dear to me, and to find a reason to live. I had realized there was more than blood, death, and the stench of war; there was *Life*—far greater than we had ever perceived it to be.

It was through this realization that I would understand, in the years to come, that man *is* the greatest of all things; and that the only reason the sun is ongoing while man dies, is that the sun never contemplates death. All it knows . . . is to be.

When I realized through contemplation who the Unknown God was, I did not wish to wither and die as the old woman had died. There must be a way, I thought, to be as ongoing as the sun.

As I continued to heal from the dire wound to my body, I had little to do but sit upon a plateau and watch my army grow fat and lazy. One day, as I looked to the horizon to see the vague outline of ghostly mountains and valleys yet uncharted, I wondered what it would be like to *be* the Unknown God, the Life Force. How could I become that ongoing essence?

That is when the wind played a jest upon me and insulted me beyond my tolerance. It blew up my cloak, which was long and regal, and dumped it on top of my head. Not a very noble position for a conqueror! Then the wind caused a wonderful pillar of saffron-colored dust to form a column beside me, all the way up into the heavens. When I was not paying enough attention, the wind ceased, allowing all the dust to fall upon me.

Then the wind went whistling down the canyon, down to where the river flowed, and on through the wonderful olive orchards, turning the leaves from emerald to silver. And it blew a beautiful maiden's skirt up around her waist—with all the giggling that went on from that. And then it blew the hat from a little child's head, and the child went racing after it, laughing gleefully.

I demanded that the wind come back to me, but it only laughed in its gales in the canyon. Then, when I was blue in the face from shouting orders, I sat back down upon my haunches . . . and it came and blew in my face, softly. "That is freedom!"

No man living would I ever have as my ideal. But as I observed the wind, it presented itself as a wondrous ideal for me. For you cannot see the wind, yet whenever it comes upon you in a fury, you are assailed. And no matter how grand and powerful you are, you cannot declare war upon the wind. What can you do to it? Cleave it with your broadsword? Spit upon it? It will only throw it back in your face.

What else could one be, I thought, that would give him such power; that could never be captivated by the limited nature of man; that would permit him to be in all places at all times; and, unlike man, that would never die?

To me, the wind was an ultimate essence, for it is magical, exploratory, and adventurous; it is ongoing, free-moving, with neither boundaries nor form. That, indeed, is the closest resemblance there is to the God-essence of Life. And the wind never judges man. The wind never forsakes man. The wind, if you call it, will come to you . . . through love. Ideals should be like that.

So I desired to become the wind. And I contemplated it for years and years. That was what *all* my thoughts were bent on becoming. I contemplated the wind and aligned myself with its elusiveness and lightness and indefinable contours. And through contemplating my becoming the wind, it was the wind that I became.

The first occurrence was not until six years after I had been run through. Every evening during that time, I would sit upon a plateau, gaze into the sky, and contemplate the wind. And there came a day, much to my surprise, when I found myself aloft in the heavens as the wind.

In but a moment I realized that I was far away from my simple speck of a body down on the plateau. When I looked down upon my embodiment, I felt fear for the first time since I had been run through. It was fear that brought me back into the body.

I opened my eyes to a cold-hot sweat over the realization that I had been outside the prison of my embodiment. I was in paradise, for I was sure that I had become the wind. I flung myself to the ground and praised God—the Source, the Power, the Cause, the Wind. Never would I forget that splendid moment when I first became the grace and beauty and bountiful life of the wind. I reasoned that what allowed me to become my ideal was my utter determination, always holding clear in thought the vision of what I wanted to become.

The next eve, I sat upon my rock, contemplated the wind with exuberant joy, and I became . . . nothing. I tried again and again and again. I knew that my experience was not simply imagination, for I had indeed seen a different perspective. I knew I had been in the air as a dove or a hawk, and had seen my pitiful self below me.

Nothing did I want, nothing did I desire, except becoming that freedom once again. But no matter how hard I struggled and how much sweat broke out upon my body (and how much cursing followed thereafter), I didn't go anywhere. I stayed right where I was.

It was two years in your time-reckoning before I became the wind again. This time it happened, not upon contemplating the wind, but upon going into a restful sleep. Before retiring, I had praised the Source, the sun, the moon, the stars, saffron dust, the sweet smells of jasmine — I praised them all! And ere I closed my lids, I was in the heavens again as the wind!

In time, I perfected the ability to leave my body. But it took an occurrence for me to understand how to go places. One day, I saw that one of my men had come into a most perilous situation. He had fallen from his horse, but his foot remained lodged in a stirrup. The moment I put my *thought* with him, *I* was with him, and I released his heel. I stood over him and wished him well, but he thought I was a dream.

I learned to travel in a moment after that, for I learned that wherever thought is, so is the thinker. And how did I conquer thereafter? I was an awesome foe, for I *knew* my enemies' thinking; thus I outwitted them all! No longer did I overthrow kingdoms; I let them overthrow themselves.

For many years I traveled in thought into other kingdoms and to other entities. And I visited civilizations in the birth of their future and lives yet unseen.

Slowly, over many years, as the thought of my ideal became the very life-force in my body, my soul gradually increased the vibratory rate within every cell. My desire was that strong! The more I identified with the wind, the more that feeling carried through my entire physical arrangement, until I became lighter and lighter and lighter. People would look at me and say, "There is a glow about the master!" There was! For my body was vibrating at a faster rate of speed—going from the speed of matter into the speed of light.

In time, my body became fainter and fainter by the light of the moon. Then, one night, I became where the moon was! No longer did I simply travel in thought; I had raised my bodily vibrations into light, and had taken my entire embodiment with me. I was gleeful and mirthful, for what I had done was unheard of! Yet I came back—but only to see if I could do it again. And I did—63 times before my final ascension.

When I became the wind, I realized how truly limited I had been and how free the elements were, for I became a wild, moving power that is free—free of weight, free of measure, free of time. I became an unseen essence that has no form, that is pulsating light, indivisible. In that, I could move with freedom through valleys and dales and glens, through mountains and oceans and stratums, and none could see me. And, like the wind, I had the power to turn leaves from emerald to silver, to move trees that are unshakable, to go into the lungs of a babe and back into the clouds to push them away.

When I became the wind, I realized how small and helpless man is in his ignorance about himself . . . and how great he becomes when he extends himself into knowledge. I learned that whatever man contemplates being, *he will become*. If man tells himself long enough that he is wretched and powerless, he will become wretched and powerless. If sees himself as being lord of the wind, he will become lord of the wind, as I did. And if he sees himself as being God, he is going to *become* God.

Once I had learned these understandings, I taught my be-

loved people for many years about the Unknown God. When I
was an old man, a day came when all I had set out to accomplish had been accomplished. So I made a journey across the
Indus river to the side of the mountain called Indus, and there
I communed with all of my people for 120 days. I urged them
to know that what I had taught them was indeed a truth; that
the source of their divine guidance was not through me or any
other man, but through the God that had created us all. For
their belief—and to their surprise—I elevated myself quite
nicely above them. Women screamed, aghast. Soldiers
dropped their broadswords in amazement. I saluted them all
farewell and urged them to learn as I had learned, to become
as I had become . . . each in his own way.

Through contemplating life elements I found more forceful
than man, more intelligent than man, that live in peaceful
coexistence beside and in spite of man, did I discover the Unknown God.

 If you ask man, "How should I look?" "What should I believe in?" "How should I live?" you will die. That *is* a truth.
Go ask the wind, "Give me knowledge, wind. Open me up
and let me know," and it will turn you from olive to silver,
take you into the hollows of the canyons, and laugh with you,
blatantly free.

 I was most fortunate in being taught by life's elements. The
sun never cursed me and the moon never said I must be a certain way. And a wonderful thing about them: in their
simplicity and steadfastness, they asked nothing of me. The
sun did not look down and say, "Ramtha, you must worship
me in order to know me." The moon did not look down and
say, "Ramtha, wake up! It is time to look upon my beauty!"
They were there whenever I looked to see them.

 I learned of the Unknown God from something that is constant, without judgment, and easily understood if man puts his
mind to it. Because of that, I was not at the hands of the
altered thinking of man—with his hypocrisy, dogma, and su-

perstitious beliefs. That is why it was easy for me to learn in my one existence on this plane what most have yet to understand—because they look for God in another man's understanding. They look for God through religious rule, through writings that they have yet to question as to *who* wrote them or *why* they were written. Man has based his beliefs, his understanding, his *life*, on something that life after life has proven itself a failure. Yet man, stumbling over his own altered thinking, imprisoned by his own arrogance, continues the steadfast hypocrisy that leads only to death.

Once I ascended, I began to know everything I wanted to know, because I went out of the density of flesh and into the fluidness of thought; in so doing, I was not inhibited by anything. Then I knew that man, in his essence, truly was God. Before I ascended I did not know there was such a thing as a soul, nor did I understand the mechanics of ascending the embodiment. I knew only that I was at peace with life and with what I had done. I had embraced life and the wonderfulness I saw in the heavens, day after day and night after night.

I learned to love myself by identifying with the power and majesty of the wind. My life became fulfilled when I took hold of all my understanding and focused it on myself. That is when peace came. That is when I began to know more. That is what allowed me to become one with the Unknown God.

It was not the wind I became, but the ideal the wind represented to me. I am now the lord over it, for I am the unseen principle that is free and omnipresent and one with all life. When I became that principle, I understood the Unknown God and all that it is—and isn't—because that is what I wanted to understand. I found the answers *within me* that allowed me to expand myself into a grander understanding.

I was Ram the Conqueror. I am now Ram the God. I was a barbarian who became God through the simplest and yet the most profound of things. What I teach you is what I learned.

***

3

Cherry Pie
And The Devil

by JZ Knight

I've had some extraordinary experiences in my life. But I'd like you to know that I was just like everyone else. When I was born, a star didn't hover over the hospital, and nobody brought me any gifts. I grew up, went to school, did very well in my career, got married, and had children. As a wife and mother, I was into having the cleanest house, the best cherry pies, and roses that would rival anyone's in the neighborhood. There just wasn't anything particularly special about me.

When I was growing up in New Mexico, I was taught in church that there was a heaven and a hell, and that somehow we were caught between the two. And I was taught to *fear* God and not to commit any sins. I wasn't even supposed to *think* about sins, because if I thought about them, I was damned. That always puzzled me, because if I sought to avoid sins, didn't I have to think about them?

A guest minister came to our church one week and preached about the "Book of Revelation," which our pastor had never

---

Prior to 1985, JZ Knight, the channel for Ramtha, would frequently greet the audience and answer questions before bringing Ramtha through her. One of the most frequently asked questions was, "How did Ramtha first come into your life?" This chapter has been edited from JZ's answers to this question on several occasions. For the complete story of JZ's life and her involvement with Ramtha, see her autobiography, *A State of Mind: My Story,* published in 1987 by Warner Books.

talked about. I tell you, his message was *terrifying* to me. This minister told us that Armageddon was coming, and he described the awful things that were going to happen to the world. He told us the earth was going to be destroyed, but before that would happen, Jesus would come back to save us, but only if we believed in him. The people who didn't believe in him would be judged, and they were going to get it—just because they didn't believe in him.

After the guest minister got through with his awful predictions, I went up to our pastor and I asked him, "Why didn't you tell us about this before?"

"Well, we always like to emphasize the *goodness* of the Father," he said.

"But why," I asked, "will God do all this to us if he *loves* us so much?" He couldn't answer my question.

There was another thing I observed at church that really disturbed me. I knew a lovely woman in our neighborhood, a very virtuous woman, and she came to one of our services wearing powder and lipstick. When she sat down, people whispered amongst themselves and called her a sinner, just because she wore make-up. Well, that really opened my eyes. That was the last time I attended church—the day they passed judgment on this very wonderful woman.

But I always loved God. Always. I was disappointed in the church because the God they talked about wasn't the God that I loved in my heart, and I felt that going to this church was a horrendous hypocrisy. So I continued to love God and continued to pray.

My life was fairly ordinary until Ramtha first came into it. It happened like this: My whole family liked to go backpacking in the mountains of Washington. When someone told my husband and I about dehydrating food using "pyramid power," my husband got very excited about trying it out as a way to lighten our backpacks. So on a Friday in early 1977, I bought several books on pyramids, some colored posterboards to make them, and a magnetic compass to align the pyramids to true north.

That night, my husband and I sat in our kitchen, cutting out triangles and taping them together. We spent the night making pyramids, aligning them with the compass, and taping them to the floor. The next day we did the same thing.

By Sunday, it was difficult to walk around the house because pyramids were *everywhere*! We had them in the hall, on the refrigerator, in the sink, in the bathroom, and under the table. We had put all sorts of things under them, including milk, bologna, and even a cockroach. We also wrote a wish on a sheet of paper and put it under one of the pyramids, thinking that it would manifest if we did that.

Sunday afternoon, the sun was just brilliant outside. My two children were over at a neighbor's house, and my husband and I were sitting in our kitchen nook with pyramids scattered about us. By that time, we were exhausted and getting pretty goofy. Well, a bit before 2:30 in the afternoon, I picked up one of these pyramids and put it on my head. I said to my husband, "If it improves food, maybe it will do something for my brains."

Laughing, my husband used the compass to align my head to true north. Then he also put one of the pyramids on his head. We were laughing so hard that tears were running down our faces.

All of a sudden, at the other end of the kitchen by the arched doorway, a light appeared. It glittered with gold and silver. The sun was shining through the glitter, which appeared to be falling very slowly. The tears in my eyes made the light appear very diffused.

I blinked and stared again at the light, and this huge male figure appeared—in broad daylight! He was so tall that his shoulders went right above the arch of the door. He had on a wonderful robe that emanated light. It was lined in a purple color, but the outside seemed to be *all* colors. Although I could see the texture of the fabric, it was light.

Do you know how women's nylons sound when they are

rubbed together? The real silk ones? They swish. Well, he stood there and his garments swished.

This entity had the most marvelous eyes. They were as deep as night, but they glowed. And he had a beautiful, broad smile, a fine chiseled nose, and a wide, firm jaw.

I was astonished! I wasn't scared. I was rather in a state of shock, because something like this just doesn't happen in a Tacoma, Washington kitchen on a Sunday afternoon!

I looked at him and said, "You're so beautiful! Who *are* you?"

A smile came upon his face, and he answered, "I am Ramtha the Enlightened One, and I have come to help you over the ditch."

"What ditch?" I thought. I immediately looked underneath my chair, and when I did, the pyramid fell over my face. As I fumbled around under the pyramid, looking for the ditch, he said, "The ditch is limited thought. I have come to teach you a better way. Prepare yourself for the greatest upbringing ever."

I looked back at him and started laughing nervously. Then he said, "Beloved woman, the greatest accomplishments are achieved with a light heart."

I didn't know what to say. I didn't know what to do! Then I started to get scared. And the moment I got scared, he faded away.

I sat there for a few moments. Then I looked at my husband, only to realize that he hadn't seen what I saw. But he *knew* something had happened. He told me that I had taken on a glow and had begun muttering things. And while that was going on, he had this very strange feeling and noticed that the compass was going crazy.

After I recounted the event to him, I started crying, because I thought I must be losing my mind! My husband, who was very excited about what had happened, tried to comfort me. Then I became *really* scared, because I remembered hearing a hell-and-brimstone revivalist say that in "the last days," the devil will appear as an angel of light to deceive the world. So I immediately thought that Ramtha was the devil.

"What's wrong with you, JZ?" my husband said, responding to the worried look on my face.

"What's wrong with *me*? What's wrong with *you*! The devil has just come to our house! What did we ever do to deserve this?"

I was mortified, and I cried out, "Do you feel good about this thing? You can't! Because if you do... *waaaah*. He's a deceiver, and... *waaaah*."

I ran upstairs, found my Bible and dusted it off, and I clutched it to my chest. I slept with it that night.

A few days later, I had lunch with the girls. They were chatting about things like, "Don't you just love the dress I have on?"... "Do you think I should get involved with what's-his-face?"... "What's going on with you, JZ?"

I didn't know what to say. "Well, I spent the weekend making pyramids, and the devil came to visit me.... I think I'll get back into religion."

A few months later, I was still bothered by this Ramtha thing. I felt I needed help, so I got out the Yellow Pages and called a church in the area.

"Hello, my name is JZ Wilder. I'm not a current member, but I was very active in Bible school when I was growing up. You see, I have this problem."

"Well, why don't you come down and we'll talk about it," the minister said. "By the way, my child, what is the nature of your problem?"

"Well, several months ago, while I had this pyramid on my head, the devil came to my house and said he'd help me over the ditch. And I don't know what to do!"

Click. He hung up on me! I called him back and I asked, "Did we have a bad connection?" And he said, "I think what you need, Mrs. Wilder," (it was no longer "my child") "is some good counseling. Don't come down. I'll have someone send you some information."

I called several churches listed in the phone book, but not one of them wanted me to come to their church. Then I reached a man named Michael at a spiritualist church. He said that his church dealt with something called "psychic knowingness," and that I could come down to talk over my situation.

"You want me to bring this to the church? It's the devil! Nobody *else* wants me to come to their church!"

"How do you know it's the devil?" he asked.

"The Bible told me it's the devil."

"It's okay. Come on down," he said.

I prettied my hair and got dressed up in my finest clothes—a yellow dress, stockings, earrings and gloves. After all, I *was* going to church!

My husband and I arrived at the church, only to find that it was a small white house located behind a bingo hall. Inside, I saw pictures of Jesus hanging on the wall. We wandered throughout the house, but no one was to be found. Eventually, we walked out into the backyard, where some men and women were eating chocolate chip cookies and drinking coffee. Michael wasn't among them, and I got pretty mad, because I really needed help, and he had promised to help me.

They were all checking us out, when I slammed my Bible down in front of them and cried out, "I don't know *who* you people are, but this is *supposed* to be a church! You *do* have Jesus hanging on the wall in there, you know! What is going *on*? Why did the devil pick *me*? I want to know, and I'm not leaving here until you tell me!"

I plopped right down in a Samsonite chair and sat there. Everyone got up except this one old woman with gray hair and wonderful eyes. She moved over next to me and said, "My name is Lorraine Graham. Tell me, what is your problem?"

I went through the whole thing about dehydrating food, the pyramids, this thing in my kitchen, and what he said to me.

"Can you *believe* that?" I said.

"Yes, I can," she replied with a knowing smile.

"Then you don't think I'm crazy?"

"No, not at all," she said. "You're just gifted."

Lorraine suggested that we go inside, where we could talk privately. After we did, she told my husband and me about mediums and how they can contact spiritual teachers in the unseen. She told us that mediums have a special gift, that they can raise the vibrational frequency of their bodies to permit a teacher to speak to them.

I only vaguely understood what she was talking about, because this was all new to me. I mean, I didn't even know what a psychic was at that time.

Well, right in the middle of my conversation with this woman, Ramtha channeled through me for the first time, but I didn't know he had come through. After Ramtha left, I resumed the conversation right where I left off. But I noticed that Lorraine had tears in her eyes, and my husband had a strange look on his face. When I asked them what was the matter, they told me that Ramtha had come through me and used my body to express himself. He had stood up, moved around, kissed Lorraine's hand, and talked to both of them.

I didn't believe them at first. I was puzzled, confused, even angry. But Lorraine was absolutely beside herself with excitement. She tried to reassure me by explaining what had happened, but I had a hard time accepting it. I wanted some proof that this whole thing wasn't crazy. So she asked us to come the next week to her home in Portland, where she had a big library of books that she said would help me to understand all of this better.

After a week of crying a lot and eating a lot, I went to Portland with my husband. When we arrived, Lorraine invited us into her tiny house, which indeed had books everywhere.

Over a cup of tea, Lorraine told me that Ramtha couldn't be the devil because there was no such thing. She explained who she thought Ramtha was, why he was doing what he was doing, and prepared me for what might happen. Then Lorraine suggested that we use her Ouija board. She took it out, and I watched as her hands started moving around the board. The first message it spelled out said that I would help teach humanity. Then it spelled the word "outside."

"Outside!" Lorraine said, as she jumped up. "I feel we must go outside immediately!"

"Outside?" This was so bizarre! Now what?

Just after we went outside, we all saw an enormous ball of light! It was absolutely quiet and hovered above the tops of the trees. Then another light appeared and split into several smaller brilliant balls of light. They were absolutely beautiful!

As I stood there in awe, my husband went over to the car and turned on the radio. A disc jockey's voice was excitedly reporting UFO sightings in the Portland area.

So, I got my proof. I went home with an armload of books and a warm regard for this woman who took me aside and taught me.

After that, Ramtha began to teach me and my family. He would appear to me *everywhere* — in restaurants, in the restroom, in the kitchen, at the grocery store, in the car. He monitored every thought we had, manifested all of our fears, and showed us our two-facedness. Can you imagine having someone monitoring your thoughts and making you look at them? It was intense! Everything I thought immediately happened right in front of me. Did I get a good look at how my thinking was creating my life!

But I was still bothered about the devil. One day, I was making a cherry pie in the kitchen when no one was around. With my apron on and my hands in the dough, I heard Ramtha come swishing in, like the wind.

"You desire to talk to me?"

"Yes, I *do* want to talk to you!"

I washed my hands, sat down at the table, and looked at him. He looked so beautiful!

"Ramtha, I don't understand why you're in my life. I love you, and I love God. But I would *die* if I thought that in my ignorance, I had betrayed Jesus. I love you, but I don't ever want to betray God.''

Ramtha looked at me and said, ''You think I am 'the evil one'?''

• ''Well, you haven't *done* anything evil. I did see you heal a woman. I saw a rose bloom when you walked by it. And I saw a Chinese pheasant appear on the patio, just as you said it would. All these things have happened, but—''

''Beloved woman, what is an 'evil one'?''

''Well, the devil doesn't love God. He was booted out of heaven because he thought he was more beautiful than God. He came to earth and he plays havoc with mankind. He tempts you to commit sins and do evil things, so he can get you in the end. Then he puts you in a pit and burns you for all eternity.''

''But why would he want to do that?'' Ramtha asked.

''Because he's evil!''

''But what does he gain by doing that? Then he'd have all of these screaming and hollering people to babysit for the rest of his life.'' Well, I'd never thought of it that way. Then Ramtha said, ''So that's the devil, eh?''

''Yes, that's the devil!''

''Beloved woman,'' he said, ''tell me what God looks like.''

''Well, um, he has a long beard. And he sits on a white throne. He wears a white gown and he has blue eyes. And—''

''Have you seen him like that?''

''Well, no, not personally.''

''So God is a man, then?''

''Well, no!''

''Beloved woman, the God that I teach you of lives in all things and *is* all things.''

''Absolutely!'' I said. ''God is all things, and he created all things.''

''So he created hell too.''

''No! He did *not* create hell! The *devil* created hell!''

''But where did the devil get the stuff to make hell from?''

''Well, you know, he just got it!''

"But *where* did he get it from?"

"I don't know."

"You agree that God is all things and all life?"

"Yes," I replied.

"Then, if there were such a place as hell, it would have to be composed of God and created by God. If you say God didn't create hell, then you're saying there's something more powerful than God who *did* create the stuff to make hell with." ♥

"Well, I don't know *what* I think anymore!"

"Beloved woman, if there were such an entity called Lucifer, then he would have to be made of God; thus the basis of his being would be pure God, meaning pure good."

"He *can't* be good!" I said.

"But he *is*, because God *made* him."

Well, that just stuck in my throat like you can't imagine. I was really stumped. Then Ramtha said, "Listen, beloved daughter, I have gone to the center of your earth seeking a fiery pit, and I didn't find anything there but a hollow center where a vast civilization of people live."

"What do you mean, it's *hollow*? That doesn't go along with anything I studied in school."

Ramtha continued. "Then I went to the edge of the universe, and I didn't find the devil there either. I went to the edge of forever, but I just found more forever. When I came back to earth, I found the devil to be alive and well in the hearts of those who *believe* in him, those who give credence to evil things. But in a greater understanding, the devil doesn't ↘ exist. He never has. He was created as a tool to enslave the entire world. The 'evil one' was created by men to cause everybody to live in fear of punishment from the devil, so that they would do whatever the Church demanded."

Ramtha helped me to reason out the devil myth. ↘I realized that I had not wanted to let go of the devil concept because I could blame him for so much. If I did a bad thing, I could always say it was the devil's fault, never my own. So I had to take full responsibility for my life the day Ramtha spoke to me in my kitchen.

After that, I became completely at ease with the Ram. I opened up my mind and I learned. I've let go of a lot of limited beliefs these past few years—sometimes kicking and screaming, because it meant letting go of my identity. But I have learned, most of all, to love myself.

Ramtha taught me for almost two years to prepare me for channeling him. On December 17, 1978, I channeled Ramtha in his first public audience.

I could go on for days telling you about Ramtha and the miracles that happened to us. But as I said, in the beginning I was very backward in my knowledge of psychics and channeling and the like. I assure you, *I* never would have gone to one of Ramtha's audiences. So I must have been Ramtha's greatest challenge. Maybe that's why he picked me—because if I could learn from him, *anyone* could.

***

JZ Knight has channeled Ramtha since 1978. "Ramtha," says JZ, "does not 'take possession' of my body. He comes around my body in the auric field and works through the chakras, the seventh energy centers in the body. I am what is termed a 'pure channel' because the whole of my essence goes to another time flow."

4

Only A Mirror

*Master:** Ramtha, I want to thank you for coming to us like this.

Ramtha: Master, I have come from no place to be here. I simply *am* here. I am pleased you have come from *your* place to be in this audience.

Master: I'm curious to know whether we create or draw to us entities such as yourself to mirror back to us our own selves? I ask that because I have listened to you, I have felt you, and yet I feel myself. Do I see you as a mirror to me? Can I see of you only what I perceive in myself?

Ramtha: That is correct.

Master: Then are you different things to different people?

Ramtha: I am everything to everyone, for I have become all things. I *am* all things. What anyone sees and perceives of me are only the things they possess within themselves. I am only a mirror that brings them forward.

Master, I have come to exalt the divinity within you and all entities. For in your innocence, you have become enslaved by the illusions and limitations of the material plane, which have become your reality. The irony is, because you are God, you are possessed with infinite power in each moment to create such illusions and limitations. When you realize that you have created your limitations through your own power and virtue,

---

*Ramtha normally addresses those who come to his audience as "master," to acknowledge that they are in the process of mastering their lives.

you will also realize that the law can work equally in the other direction—that you hold within yourself the power to create unlimitedness.

You allowed yourself to be all that you are. You, an unseen enigma, chose to be immersed in a river of limitation in order to experience and learn about it. For those who are lost in it and are desiring to become unlimited once again, I am a beacon for the way back home, for I have experienced all that you have experienced and learned to transcend the illusions of the material plane. No one can truly help mankind unless they have been man and learned how to unsnare themselves from the dream of limitation.

In the frequency of thought that I have become, you can be and experience anything you desire. The more you become yourself, the more you will be as I am. You already *are* what I am. All that remains is to *realize* that—by *loving* yourself, embracing *all life*, and knowing that life, in its totality, is *wholly* beautiful; that it is only one's attitude toward life that makes it a wretched thing. And *who* is the creator of such an attitude? The individual who accepts it.

Master, you have completed much on this plane and you have become grand in your knowingness. The only thing that remains for you to accomplish here is creating the experiences that will allow you to see who you truly are. I am here to help you see that, for you have *desired* to see that. I am here, not to *teach* you of who you are, but to help you create the experiences through which you will teach yourself.

You can tell entities only so much. You cannot *make* them realize their divinity. You can tell them where to look, but how can they gain the emotional understanding unless *they* do the looking? The Will sees only what it *desires* to see.

In my one existence here, I learned greatly, and I came to understand life in its basis. All I had to do was *look*. Once I had taught my people all I had learned, I had no thing left to accomplish or gain from this plane of understanding. My knowledge kept wanting . . . more! I knew there was more, and I went in search of it. And I tell you, master, there is *indeed* more, and I am completely taking it all in.

When you come to my audiences, what you hear are the same talks I gave my people long ago. The reality of living as man has changed very little since then. Fashion has changed, technology has changed, but not living. I am teaching you the same understandings I taught you many years ago, for now you are ready to learn. Those who come to these audiences desiring to look, they will learn, greatly; and that knowingness, that *emotional* understanding, will take them into a kingdom of joy that cannot be described by any words on your plane.

Master, I love what you are, deeply. For what you are, I am also. And I will teach you to see hope, hope that extends your life into greater understanding.

Master: Thank you, Ramtha.

Ramtha: Love yourself, master. Loving yourself is the only way to bring forth the infinite within you, the god within. Love yourself into life, into joy, into God. I will continue to mirror to you your own truth, your own beauty, your own is-ness. And when self is fully seen and known, you will be able to help others better understand who *they* truly are behind their masks, merely by casting their eyes upon *you*.

I am pleased you have desired to look and have humbled yourself to listen to such as I. I love you greatly. So be it.

***

5

Allow Them To Choose

Master: (A close friend of JZ) Ramtha, I'm curious as to why you have chosen to speak to us through JZ?

Ramtha: Why have I brought forward this illusion? For only in this manner can I interact with you so that I might speak to you, embrace you, and help you.

Master: But why did you choose to speak to us through the body of a woman?

Ramtha: Ah! You see, master, God, the intelligence, the sublime emotion, is both man *and* woman. If I appeared to you as a man in order to bring forth the understanding of who God truly is, many would continue to see God as being male. If I manifested myself as a woman, many would say, "Aha! God is the *Mother* of the Universe!" And if I appeared in my light body, everyone would be so awed, they would never listen, but would worship me instead.

My daughter was a babe when I came up with the idea to come through her. I watched her grow, and I helped her grow. Because she had a great love for God and a wondrous desire to help everyone, I knew that one day, I could teach her of all that I am, and that between the two of us we could do something very constructive upon this plane.

My plan has worked very well. When I come forth, you see a woman but you hear a man: the two representing the "one," which is God, the Isness. And the knowledge and wisdom you

45

hear comes forth in great emotion, which is pure God.

Master: Also, what is the purpose of the deep breathing you do when you first enter JZ's body?

Ramtha: It is done to open her chakras,* to expand them. And I do not *enter* my daughter's body, I am *around* it, in the auric field of the body's molecular structures. That is how I use her body to perpetrate this illusion you see before you.

Master: Could you explain to me why JZ's body swells up and retains water when you are using it?**

Ramtha: Water is a conduit for electricity. When I come forth, greater water is needed for the electrical flow of my vibratory frequency. So, whatever fluids my daughter has taken into her body will be held there to maintain the necessary energy level while this work is being done. That is what causes the swelling. If the water was not held, this seal *(pointing to the throat area, the location of the fifth seal)* would not expand to allow me to speak through this woman I love.

The swelling that occurs is a misery to my daughter, who finds it embarrassing, uncomfortable, and not at all lovely. She complains that I distort her face—that I *mash* it. Well, I suppose I do. But when all is said and done, she is very pleased, for when she returns she sees wonderfulness all around her.

In the beginning of this work, her body could not hold my vibration; thus the body was very restrictive, and would tear profusely from the eyes and mouth. I was without movement, very stiff and anchored. I did not have bodily expression, only words from the fifth seal. If I expressed great emotion, this seal "erupted," and shortly thereafter, my daughter was unable to speak for long periods.

I have gradually made the body more attuned for this work, for as my daughter's body becomes more, I am allowed to express greater.

*The body has seven glands or energy centers that have been called chakras or seals.
**This question was asked in an audience in 1981, when JZ's body swelled up greater than it currently does.

Master: Ramtha, I'm concerned about the length of time you use JZ's body. I know of other channels, but I've never known any who channel for as many hours as JZ does. I trust that you know how to adjust the frequency of her body so that it is not thrown out of balance.

Ramtha: Indeed. I have to, or I could not do this work. And this woman is indeed a rarity, master, for how many would allow this occur for the length of time she does, permitting these moments of her life to escape her.

Master: But are those moments really lost? Since nothing in the universe is lost, aren't those moments merely delayed?

Ramtha: They are not recognized. You see, upon this plane, there is a reckoning of measurement. But where my daughter goes, there is neither time nor distance. When she comes back into the heaviness of the body, she does not have conscious memory of what has occurred in these audiences. That is done as a protection for her. For being a sensitive entity, she has great compassion for everyone, and could not tolerate knowing much of what occurred here.

Master: But isn't what is said in your audiences important for her own evolutionary process as well?

Ramtha: Oh, entity, where she is this moment, she is evolving, I assure you. For I send her to my kingdom, which is a totally unlimited consciousness.

You see, if you take an entity out of social consciousness—where the prevalent mode of thinking is guilt, fear, judgment, and living for the sake of others—and we put the entity in an unrestrictive consciousness, where all is joy, where there is a peace that passeth all understanding, the entity will advance greatly. Each moment my daughter is in that consciousness, she is learning. Each time she returns, she comes back lifted in her being, in her knowingness, greater and greater.

Master: Thank you, Ramtha. As you know, I'm writing another book about my life. In it, I plan to include my experiences with you and other channeled entities. How can I make your teachings acceptable to people who doubt the process of channeling, because they think it's really JZ speaking from her unconscious or her higher self?

Ramtha: You cannot, master, because each entity will accept only what he *wants* to accept. And most will accept only what is in accordance with the understandings of their families, peers, or society. They will not entertain any understanding that will disrupt their comfort zones. They want their lives to be nice and tidy.

Master: Yet many people, especially my intellectual friends, are telling me they don't *want* life to be tidy. Accepting you and what you teach would *make* life tidy. It would tie up with a blue ribbon all of the questions about God and life and love and all that harmony stuff, which they think is—

Ramtha: Master, it doesn't tie up *anything* until *they* experience it. What are *words*? What are teachings, after all? They are only dry philosophy until they are experienced. What I teach you is only conjecture until it has been *felt*.

Accepting me and the understandings I give forth wouldn't tidy up *anything*! It would cause their lives to go into great havoc. For then they would have to wholly own up to the responsibility for their lives; they would have to learn to feel deep love, to feel great compassion; they would have to learn to *feel*, which is wholly without intellect or logic. And in order to understand this God of whom I teach, which is the totality of everything that exists, they would have to *become* it, in *emotion*. That does not make their lives tidy, not at all. That takes them a long way from their limited identity and cloistered selves.

Their questioning my reality does not bother me, master. When they are ready to experience love and life, they will open up and listen, because that will have become the most important thing to them.

Master: What I don't understand is why people won't at least take a look. Why are they so closed to channeling before they have even experienced the phenomenon?

Ramtha: Tell me, master, why do people believe in their religions and dogmas, yet they have never experienced the reality of what they believe?

Master: Because they were taught it every Sunday.

Ramtha: That is correct. And through those teachings they have been programmed to guard against anything that brings them a different truth. If they were taught every *Thursday* to be open to truth, regardless of the source, they would be open to perceive the reality that I am.

Master: So how do you tell someone that it's wise to be open-minded? How do you get that across?

Ramtha: You don't do that! You simply say what is a truth for you, and allow others to accept it or not. Do have the grace, entity, to allow them to choose. You wish to have the whole of the world accept me, or others like me? I tell you, you are acting like a tyrant and an enslaver! Allow them to believe whatever they *want* to believe. Allow them the privilege, master, to experience and learn from their thinking. There will come a time in their lives when they will *want* to know, and they will be drawn to seek out a grander understanding. And it will be there for them when they do.

I say to you, my beloved brother, just as you sit in this audience, *many* will be sitting here in the times to come. Already, many all over your world are seeking what you are hearing, because they *want* to know.

You have a great "enemy," as you term it, called the Country of the Bear. Do you know how they are getting their knowledge? Through entities such as I who channel forth wisdom. That is how they are becoming grand in their scientific understandings.

Master: So you're saying that channeling is more sophisticated in the Soviet Union than it is here?

Ramtha: Indeed. The young ones of that country have a greater advantage of exploring with their minds than those in your country, for here, most are brought up to fear and doubt that which is unseen. Their youth are feeling the power of unlimited thought, and that openness to knowledge is used by their government to bring forth technological advances in their scientific programs.

Master: But Ramtha, if entities such as you are helping them develop their technology, won't they become a greater military threat to this country?

Ramtha: Master, do you know the wondrous thing that happens when an entity opens up and begins to expose himself to knowledge? Soon he knows so much that he loses the desire to conquer. He realizes the power he has, and does not need to *convince* himself of it by conquering others. He realizes that nothing on this plane is limited, and that whatever he desires, he does not have to take from another entity, for he knows he can manifest it in a moment. You see?

Now, in answer to your question, master: Those who choose not to come into my audience stay away because it is safer not to come here.

Master: Because hearing you would upset preconceived ideas, and they would have to change, and they sense that?

Ramtha: That is correct.

Master: So they are already *sensing* this force you represent?

Ramtha: That is correct.

Master: So they are already *admitting* your reality by being afraid of it?

Ramtha: That is correct.

Master: I didn't need to ask you these questions, did I?

Ramtha: That is, indeed, correct.

Master: Thank you, Ramtha.

Ramtha: Master, do not concern yourself over those who are not yet ready to listen to what is being said in these audiences. That is not true of the whole. There is not a man, woman, or child who has not had a memory of another time, another place, that they have wondered about. All have felt and experienced unexplained things, and many of them want understand; they are eager for knowledge, master. Put down on papyrus what you know, and what you put down *many* will purchase in the marketplace. And what you say will ring true within their souls. And they will love you grandly for setting an example of being bold enough to speak your truth, regardless of those who would ridicule you for it.

I am pleased you have come to this audience. I desire for you to have compassion for those who hide their emotions behind the facade of their intellect. For a day is coming very soon when they will experience a great inner battle, a deep humbling, but also a grand release into life. So be it.

***

6

Bored With Life

Ramtha: (To a young man) Master, what say you?

Master: Well, I really don't have any questions to ask you. Actually, I have mixed emotions about being here. A friend told me about you and how meaningful it is to come to your audience. But frankly, I find this all pretty boring. I haven't heard anything I don't already know, only a bunch of glib answers to some petty problems. At times I think that everybody here has got to be absolutely insane for being here.

Ramtha: Then why do you stay?

Master: That's a good question. I think it's because I keep waiting to hear something that applies to me.

Ramtha: Master, never go against your feelings and stay with something that bores you, when you could be experiencing life and its adventures. If you are bored, and yet you stay, you are living in a state of great duality and disharmony, which one should never do. If you are bored, you should certainly go from this place, straightaway, and find a challenge that brings you joy. To stay with something that bores you is being a fool. If you wish to express as a fool, be happy to be known as that, and do not complain.

Master: It wasn't meant to be a complaint. I was only expressing my feelings.

Ramtha: On the contrary, master, you have expressed your opinion, wondrously well. Had you truly been expressing your feelings, I dare say you would be a most enlightened entity.

Now, as long as you have found that it suits your divided self to remain, in the hope that perchance I would impart unto you words of great wisdom that would be applicable to your life, I will tell you this: The reason you say you are bored here is that it gratifies your ego to say that, for it gives you a feeling of importance and superiority. You feel good in being the only one in this audience who doesn't feel there is something to be gained here, because that means you are unique. But I tell you, master, in the substance of your being you're no different from anyone else—and you *never* will be. You are neither greater nor less than anyone here, because in the totality of what you are, you are God, as everyone here is. That is what gives you and every other entity the power to create your opinions however you choose.

You are just like everyone else. And you're as *important* as everyone else is. If you wish to stay and listen, by all means do so. But do part this audience straightaway if it devastates your character to listen to the enigma that I am and to the "poor, wretched creatures" who are here. I love you too greatly to encourage you to stay, entity, and wish not for you to continue living an hypocrisy because you cannot humble yourself enough to love the beauty I see in you.

Master: (After long silence from Ramtha) It seems like you stopped in the middle of a statement, and that there was more you were going to say.

Ramtha: I'm afraid, master, it would only *bore* you.

Master: Perhaps it will, but I'd like to hear it anyway.

Ramtha: Master, I will tell you this: You will never know the joy I know, nor will you ever experience the unlimited freedom I have found, until you go beyond your fear and stubborn intellect to love yourself and the whole of humanity. You see, what *bores* you has bridged me into forever. For the reward of love is the beginning of eternity.

I have mended broken hearts, healed diseased and dying entities (characters you would call boring). I have kissed feet you would never touch. I have held entities rotted with cancer and wiped away the vileness of their wounds, whose stench you couldn't bear. I have listened to the deep despair of entities who never found anyone else to share it with. Why do I these things? Because there is no greater gift than to see an innocent creature, enslaved and hurt by things you find unimportant, come out of his illusions to find himself, to see his own magnificence, to become what no other would allow him to become.

I do not have to do this, I *want* to. Because there is no greater feeling than having the freedom in your being to express love to every entity, and to help them realize that they are loved by God regardless of how they are expressing. What each of those who come here are, master, *I am*, and I have the ability to be judgeless, and the compassion, humility, and love to be a catalyst that allows them to find their own joy.

How many times have I been asked by simple innocents the same questions, over and over again? Yet I never tire of the vibrance of humanity and the God that lives fervently within all entities. Each entity who asks, and then listens, is hearing something he has never heard from anyone else. And he learns that there are no ideals he need be or become other than the beauty he *already* is. What I teach *is* boring, for there is no glamour or fear in it; there are no rules, rituals, regulations, or dogmas.

What am I doing here? Nothing, except being love, which never ends, *never*. Each moment I am that, the greater life becomes, for love is the power that supports *all life*. That is a grand reality you have yet to see. That understanding will change the entire consciousness on your plane and bring to it its greatest freedom.

For you to love yourself, master, would be too humiliating. Yet you are so starved for love that you will frustrate yourself to get it. That is why a day is coming when you will feel a terrible pain in your body. And your arm will become an extension of that pain. The pain will well up in your throat, your tongue will roll backward, and you will begin to choke. You will begin to hurt so badly that you will collapse right where you are, for the terror of the unseen assassin has encompassed your entire being.

You are now lying there, desperately gasping for breath, your vision a blur. People are rushing around in great confusion, and they are yelling something at you, but their voices seem so far, far away.

As you are rushed to the infirmary, in great desperation and immense agony, you feel an erratic movement in your heart. And you cannot breathe fast enough or deep enough to calm it and hold on to your life.

As they send a great current to your heart to keep it steadfast, you are *amazed* at the energy of the entities around you, battling to extreme measures to keep you alive. And you wonder why in the world they would care so much about you.

They are now looking down into your eyes and asking, "Can you *hear* us?" But their voices are muffled and their faces distorted, blurred by the panic and the tears in your eyes.

Your mind begins to race with thoughts: "Where are all the sounds? What was it my mother used to say to me? Don't go out in the street. Stay away from strangers!" Smells of things you've long forgotten come to mind. The faces of all who said they loved you flash before you; how odd you never really looked into their eyes before, never truly noticed them. And you picture all the things you've taken for granted . . . flowers that bloom in early morn, children engaged in play, wildfowl in flight to another place. Don't they know you hurt so bad? And you think about all of the shoulds and should nots, the teachings, the beliefs, the traditions, and how they don't mean anything now. And through the pain and frantic fear, your soul begins to weep, and weep, and weep.

As hopelessness and sorrow permeate your entire being, your heart becomes even more erratic. So they plunge things down your nose and throat, slice open your chest, and desperately try to make you hold on.

The last thing you remember is how bright everything becomes, how distant the voices are, and the great silence you can almost hear. And in a moment, entity, you will be no more upon this plane.

Where go you who are starved for love? To a place where everyone around you starves for love, and there you will ponder yourself and your life. And a great entity will appear, who will teach you of the magnificence of self, so clearly that you'll wonder why you never saw it before. And you will weep ten thousand tears. When you have shed all the tears you never allowed yourself to shed before, and felt all the feelings you never allowed yourself to feel before, there will be a new zeal within you to experience and feel *more* . . . life!

One day, master, you will come back to this plane, and you will be an entity whom everyone says is divine. For you will weep when you see a rose, or the sun rising like a great fireball over stately mountains. And you will be humbled as you sit at the base of a great tree. And you will hold everyone in awe and respect, and have great love and compassion for them. For all of the emotions that were once boring have taken on a different meaning, and you will revel in them.

When you leave this plane after that existence, master, you will leave because you want to. And you will never have to prove anything to yourself or anyone else, ever again.

Do you know why the heart fails? Because the soul has not been permitted to engage itself in the expression of love and life, which are one and the same.

(After brief pause) This is *not* your doom, master. Nor is it your plight alone, no more than it is anyone else's who denies his feelings.

Learn to listen to your feelings and to honor them, so that you engage love into life, so that you engage joy into it. Have enough consideration for yourself to live what you truly feel. Then you will never come to circumstances that bring unhappiness and displeasure to your being, such as this day in my audience has brought you. Then you will regret nothing on this plane, and your beautiful heart, which you also take for granted, will continue as a happy organism without illness or disease.

What is the desire of the all-wise, knowing intelligence for you? Whatever makes you happy. For when you are happy, you add to the joy of all life. If the Father *desires* that for you, perhaps you should honor his wish and learn how to always be that way.

Stay in my audience if you wish, but depart if it pleases you not. Do whatever makes you happy. No matter what you do, it does not change how you are seen and known and loved. So be it, lord.

***

7

Sleeping Cinderellas

Master: I am very concerned about two of my daughters. They are . . . well, they're like Cinderellas. They sleep.* They don't sleep literally; they sleep in their lives. It's like they don't *live*.

For one of my daughters, it seemed like her Prince Charming had come. But then he was killed in an avalanche two years ago, and she doesn't feel she will ever again find someone to love her—and for her to love. And she *sleeps*.

My other daughter lives in a kind of apathy. She has a lover, but he lives with his mother, and he's sick all the time. So after 10 years it has come to nothing. And, and . . . I grieve for my daughters. And . . . I feel guilty.

Ramtha: Entity, what be a Cinderella?

Master: Cinderella was a girl in a fairy tale. When she was born, the good fairies came and gave her beauty and intelligence and a loving heart. But the bad fairy hadn't been asked to come—or the invitation came late. So when she got there, she was very angry, and she said that when Cinderella reached a certain age—I can't remember what it was—she would prick her finger with a needle from a spinning wheel, and would fall asleep. And everybody in the castle would also fall asleep. When Cinderella grew up, everything the bad fairy

---

*The woman has confused the story of Cinderella with that of Sleeping Beauty.

said would happen, happened. But then a young prince came, and he managed to get through the bushes with big thorns that had grown up all around the castle. Oh, yes! And he kissed her, and she woke up, and the whole castle woke up too! And everybody lived happily ever after.

So, I see two of my daughters as Cinderellas. You know, they're asleep!

Ramtha: But entity, why worry you, when the Prince is still to come and wake them up?

Master: But I'm still *waiting* for the Prince! One of my daughters is 33, the other is 30. I know this is silly, but it's as if their lives are passing them by.

Ramtha: Perhaps *your* life is passing *you* by, and you are living it through your Cinderellas.

Master: Well, that's what I thought for a while, but in the last year, many things have happened to me that have been *great*. I'm doing all the things I wanted to do when I was young. I'm really very happy. So my life is going on and getting better, but they're just sleeping theirs away.

Ramtha: Master, how long did *you* slumber until you were awakened?

Master: Sixty-two years.

Ramtha: Entity, what gives you the right to take the advantage of slumbering away from them? You are acting like an enslaver.

Master: But I don't *want* them to wait 62 years!

Ramtha: Master, it is not *your* life. It is their own!

Master: I know that.

Ramtha: You do *not* know that! If you did, you would allow them the freedom to express according to what gives them happiness. Who is to say what the guise of happiness is? Illness is a happiness to some, sorrow is a happiness to others, reclusiveness to yet someone else, and slumber, sweet slumber, a happiness to yet others.

You are *not* your children, master, nor are they you! They are sovereign entities. Though they are born of your womb, they are gods who have been created of God alone. They have not come into this life to *please* you and to live for *your* approval. They came here for *themselves*, for the opportunity to create their own lives according to what *they* see as happiness.

Master, your priority in life is never going to be anyone else's. If it has taken you 62 years to come alive, how wonderful it is that you did so. How wonderful! If one experiences that only for a moment, the whole of that lifetime has been worth it.

Allow your Cinderellas to be Cinderellas. They, like everyone else in your blessed world, are doing what makes them happy, or they would not be doing it.

Master: But they don't *seem* happy.

Ramtha: Who are you to say that? Are you living in such a state of omnipresence that you can see within the thoughts and feelings of others to determine that?

Master: I'm not sure what you mean.

Ramtha: Master, no one knows the soul of another. No one knows what experiences another needs to grow in their understanding of life and to evolve into grander and grander happiness.

Every entity is evolving. They are expanding out of their own awareness, their own understanding, into a greater awareness. Each moment, they choose for themselves, out of their awareness, what they most need to experience. And only *they* know what that is for themselves.

Master: Yes, I see that. But I guess what's bothering me is that they look sad, and I don't want to feel that sadness. So I want them to look happy—or to *be* happy.

Ramtha: Lady, then you are taking away their right to experience and understand sadness.

What you see as "unhappiness" could only be seen because you have been that and you learned of a grander happiness. But *they* do not see it that way; unto their beings, they are well and good. You are the only one who thinks otherwise. That you have learned of happiness is wonderful! But do give them the grace to learn of that on their own.

Lady, I have realized a joy and a happiness that you have yet to even *contemplate*. But am I saddened in my being for what you have yet to realize? I am not, master, for you are living how you need and desire to live, and you are evolving, you are growing, you are moving into total joy. All are.

Allow your daughters to gracefully grow into their own understanding and their own wisdom, as you have. Allow them to determine and find happiness for their own beings. That is what this life is for. Do you think this is the *only* life they are going to live?

Lady, mind your own business and love yourself. Go frolic and enjoy this place, and do all things that bring merriment and zest to your being. Love your children and give them the freedom to express however they choose. In that, you will find this life to be even sweeter than you now think it to be. That is what I say unto you.

Master: Will they find . . . I know this is my—

Ramtha: Will they find happiness according to *your* opinion?

Master: No! Will they find *husbands*!

Ramtha: Master, when entities go *looking* in the marketplace for a husband, they often settle for a bargain. And bargains very rarely hold up. Don't ever desire that your daughters *find* husbands. Desire that whatever they are will draw to them reflections of what they are. Then they won't live with a bargain, but will indeed experience a love and a sharing that will last them forever.

Leave them alone and love them in freedom. That is what I have to say to you. So be it.

***

8

Eye Of The Needle

Ramtha: Master, what desire you?

Master: (Choking back tears) I've had to live this lifetime with everybody telling me—or maybe me telling myself—that having money is bad; that if you're going to go the spiritual route, you shouldn't have money, because that's not right. But I would really like a home and some of the more desirable things in life. I drew up a plan for what I want to do, and I had a lot of fun doing that. I hadn't had such fun in a long time. And . . . *(tears welling in his eyes)* I'd like to go through with it. Can you help me?

Ramtha: Entity, what I teach all to understand is that truth is optional, and that all are gods who create truth according to their freedom of will. What you have been told and have *accepted* as your truth is a belief someone invented because he was impoverished and was jealous of the rich man.

Everything that exists in this kingdom is God, is it not? For if something were not God, it would exist outside of God, and God would not be the allness that everyone deems him to be. Correct?

Master: Yes.

Ramtha: Thus, what is termed gold, or money, is also God, is it not?

Master: That would make sense.

Ramtha: And the trees that are forged into pulp to make the papyrus that makes your dollars is also God, is it not?

Master: Yes.

Ramtha: Then, applying pure reason, why would it be bad to have God—and a *lot* of him? *(Audience laughs and applauds.)*

There is nothing wrong with having money, for you cannot separate money from God. Money is simply a means of exchanging energy in order to do and have those things that bring fulfillment to your being. And are not the things you desire to have, also a part of God's kingdom?

Master: Yes. I never thought of it that way.

Ramtha: Do you not think that God desires you to experience *all* that he is?

Master: Yes, I guess he would.

Ramtha: I will tell you a great truth: The Church has been a form of great tyranny, because it has suppressed people and kept them ignorant for many centuries. Through its dogma, it has taught that to find God, you cannot be the rich man. This teaching has been a very clever design to give great power to the Church. If you keep a man suppressed by removing his treasury, giving him a little ground to work, and then forcing him to give the best of his yield to the Church, you will always have dominion over him, always. Then man, the god, the creature birthed in freedom to live in freedom, becomes man the enslaved, man the wretched. That plan has worked very well, but has also been a great atrocity, for this teaching has been passed on to many generations.

When you, wondrous man, are freed from the fear of not having enough bread to eat, of not having a hovel to shelter and protect you, or steeds to transport you, then you can live in freedom, for then your mind is not preoccupied with the struggle to survive. Then you are happy and you have the peace of mind that allows you to receive greater, more unlimited thoughts. That is how joy is born. That is how genius and brilliance enter into your thinking processes. And when you have become these things, what is it that you have become, which honors and exalts your Father who has given you all of these things? You have *become* the Father—joy! freedom! unlimited thought! Then you can take your joy and your genius, and you can create a greater means of pleasure and freedom for all who wish to participate in your creations. Then you lift the consciousness of all who observe your life, for they will look upon you and say, "He is, indeed, a rich man, but he can go through the eye of a needle."

Entity, there are no degrees of God's love. God loves the rich man the same as he loves the pauper, the same as he loves the priest or the murderer. And there are no degrees of being spiritual, for spirit is everything, which is God, the Isness.

Whatever you want, you will have, and the doors will open to you so that you may build your kingdom on a great and wondrous foundation. And one day, lord, when all your majestic dreams have come true and you have fulfilled yourself in this kingdom of God, you will desire to become infinite, for you will have fully experienced this plane and will desire a new adventure into life.

To become God and all that comprises his being, you must allow yourself to experience everything that God is, be it riches or poverty, joy or hatred. You can never become the sovereign if you deny yourself any feeling you desire to experience. That is a great truth. You understand?

Master: Yes. Thank you.

Ramtha: Draw your plans as grandly as you can imagine, for you will always have what you envision and what you feel you deserve. When the doors open, go through them. They will be little doors in the beginning, but they will lead to greater and greater ones. When you have accomplished all of these things, rich man, give thanks to the Father within you and bless all that you have. And never feel guilty for having abundance, for that is partaking of God and his wondrous kingdom. So be it.

***

9

If This
Isn't Heaven

Master: Ramtha, I have a horse that's very dear to me, and I'd like to know, is there a heaven for animals?

Ramtha: What think you heaven to be, wondrous entity? What is your ideal of heaven?

Master: It is a wonderful place where God and all good people are. And I hope to get there one of these days—not very soon, though!

Ramtha: Master, what do you call where you are now?

Master: Well, it's not exactly heaven.

Ramtha: Why is it not?

Master: At least, I don't think it is.

Ramtha: Lady, have you ever looked into the depths of a red rose and smelled its wonderful aroma?

Master: Yes.

Ramtha: Have you ever looked at how blue a bluebell is?

Master: Yes.

Ramtha: Have you ever touched a wonderful tree, blooming with emerald leaves and fervent blossoms, and seen bees humming around it, and sap running out of it, and ants crawling around the sap?

Have you ever watched the tree lose its blossoms to the budding fruit that start very small, grow and grow and grow, and then, saying *nothing*, ripen beautifully in the sun? And soon, they fall to the ground, and a horse comes by and eats one. And the tree stands there, proud in its sweet nurturing, and whispers in the summer breeze, "We have done well."

Soon, you wake up one morning and you notice that the air has a different smell, and that it is blowing from a different direction. You feel a nip in the morning air and see a frosty glistening upon the grass. And you look at the tree as it begins to shiver, and you see the beautiful leaves, which have turned in their color, begin to fall.

Soon, you look out one morning and you see there is but one leaf, high upon the tallest branch, barely hanging on. As you look at it, a wind comes up and blows, the tree begins to shake, and the last little leaf falls gently between the branches and lands upon a bough. Then the wind comes again and it blows the leaf, and the leaf ripples to the ground.

Soon, you go out again and touch the tree, and you see that it is cold, through and through. And you say, "This tree must have died! For look, whatever happened to the blossoms and the bees, and the emerald leaves and the fruit, and the horse that ate the fruit, and the last golden leaf—where did they go?" And the tree, naked in its beauty, only shivers as a cold winter wind whistles through its branches.

Soon, you awake one morning and see that a great white stillness has fallen upon the land. As it lies in the boughs and glistens brightly, on that same branch where the leaf once was, you see an icicle of crystalline beauty, hanging there.

Soon, you arise one morning, when all of the snow is gone and the wind smells a little sweeter, and you go out and look at the wonderful tree. And you see that it is like an im-pregnated woman, bulging on every branch with budding new life. And soon it will have the leaves, and the blossoms, and the bees again . . .

If this isn't heaven—watching life recur in the beauty of its seasons—if this isn't God, there is no place you will *ever* find him. God *is* the rose in its deep color and splendid aroma. You can even smell him. And he can change, miraculously, from flower, to fruit, to golden leaf, to barrenness, to death . . . all the way back into life again. His secrets are openly simple. He is as much here as any place else.

This, lady, is heaven too. For what is heaven? Life! Heaven is feeling life and its amazing beauty.

The horse that ate the apple, he is like the tree. When the last breath goes out of him, it is like the last leaf that falls. And where goes he in his winter? To heaven, every time. And he will return again, for new foals in the spring are those who have died in the winter.

Animals have their heaven also. They have a soul and spirit, as do even the minutest of life forms. And they go through all of their seasons, just as the tree does, as the rose does, as everything else blooms and goes through its changes.

Find a tree and watch it. Seek out a rose and look upon it. If you look carefully, truly *seeing* the magic and the beauty of these things, you will have known God in his wondrous simplicity.

The tree comes back in the spring. So does the steed . . . and so will you.

***

10

Marriage Of The Soul

Master: Ramtha, I would like to do something to make myself happy. I've had an unhappy marriage for a number of years.

Ramtha: I am aware, entity.

Master: I would like to leave this marriage, and I need your help to know how to tell my husband and my children that I plan to leave very soon.

Ramtha: It will not be so difficult, entity, if you continue to remind yourself of the reason you are doing it. The reason is self-happiness. You have lived long enough in the shadow of other people's desires. Now it is time to live for self.

Master, the only way ever to speak to another is in complete love, but "evenly." To speak "evenly" is to earnestly express how you feel, but in compassion. If you love yourself, you will do this straightaway. And if they are hurt, it is because they *want* to be hurt; that is their choosing. Their expectancy that you will be a certain way all of your existence is quite enslaving, when God changes *every moment*.

The only person who will be with you forever is you. Think about why you are wanting this and then do it.

Master: Ramtha, I would also like to re-marry. I have met someone who I would like to marry, and I wonder when would be the best time for us to do this.

Ramtha: Why do you want to do that?

Master: I want to marry someone I love and someone who loves me—and someone who will not make me feel that I am a servant, as I have felt for the past 29 years.

Ramtha: Will you do, perhaps, what I tell you to do?

Master: I'll think about it.

Ramtha: That is a wise answer. Master, do *not* marry him. You are already married in your soul by the mere fact that you desire this union. And who can sanctify the marriage of the soul? Your government doesn't even know where the soul is located!

Do not marry him. If you do, you will have lessened and placed a limitation upon that which is already pure and virtuous. Go and live together and be happy in the moments that you share with each other.

Master: Ramtha, I don't know if I can live with someone without marrying him.

Ramtha: Why? Because you do not have a document that says you are married?

Master: Probably so.

Ramtha: Master, what can you possibly do in your reality that you have not first done in your thoughts? If you fantasize living with your man and copulating with him—*which you do*—you have *already* done it. You wish to sanctify it to make it acceptable? Only you can give acceptance to your life.

You are not marrying for approval and acceptance! You are marrying for passion and love—which have *nothing* to do with papers! And to sanctify it in the name of God—in the name of God it has *already* been sanctified, for love and desire do that. The only thing that sanctifies the union of two entities is *emotion*, and that is already there.

(After pause) Entity, tell me what your vows are for marriage. Speak them to me.

Master: "To love, honor, and obey." Is that what you mean?

Ramtha: And that *indeed* is the thing that got you into trouble all of these years. You committed to being a servant, and so you have been.

The *greatest* marriage, master, is the marriage of soul. The marriage of soul commits to nothing except feelings. It doesn't vow to do *anything*; it simply *is*, and it lives each moment according to desire and fulfillment. That is the purest love there is, the purest desire, the purest passion. When you love that way, you will have the grandest happiness every moment, which can then be shared with another entity.

Don't mar your love. Don't chain it. Be kind to your being. Love yourself grandly enough to let yourself flow with your feelings each moment. And don't marry the man just to please him. Remember, you are trying to get out of living that way.

That is my answer. If you love yourself and you earnestly wish to experience true happiness, you will not marry this entity. You will go and be happy with the man that you love, and you will find your bliss, wonderfully. So be it.

(Seeing that the woman still looks troubled) God will never judge you, you know.

Master: But everyone *else* would!

Ramtha: And who are *they*? Not one of them will *die* for you! If they will not take your place to save you from dying, why should you care, entity, what they think of your living?

Master: It's very thought-provoking.

Ramtha: It is indeed, master. And if you contemplate this further, you will realize that the only opinion *ever* deserving gratification is yours, and that no one else really cares about *your* life; all they care about is their own. And that is *wonderful*, for that is how they should be.

The next time someone is very hasty in their judgment of your actions, contemplate for a moment whether this person who is making a mockery of your existence would kindly die for you. If he would not, bless him from the lord-god of your being, and send him on his way.

Everyone thinks that God is full of laws and regulations and all of that. Well, he isn't. He hasn't got the time. He is too busy enjoying what he is.

***

11

Soulmates

Ramtha: (Raises his glass of lemon water) To the bitter water.
It is a cleanser of the body, and it represents the dissolution of
limited thought—that which does not *allow* knowledge to
come forth. *(Toasts the audience)* To Life!

*Audience Members: (Holding up their glasses of lemon
water)* To Life! *(All drink)*

Ramtha: I am the *outrageous* Ramtha, and I am pleased that
you have come here this day in your time.

*(Models JZ's white sports outfit, the top of which is laced
with rhinestones)* Contemporary, eh? It is called glitter, and
I . . . glitter! Well, it is to change, perhaps, your notion of
what angels are supposed to look like.

(After surveying the audience) This is a wondrous gathering. We have here a collage, a mixture of entities who are here
for different reasons. There are those of you who have come
here to find your soulmates. Then there are those of you who
are here because you're, ah, curious. And there are many of
you who were here at the last Soulmates Intensive. Didn't get
enough? Need more runners, eh?

So, you're a collage. You are that which makes up the human drama on this plane. But what each of you truly is, is a
grand god. Most of you don't know that so well, but eventu-

Excerpted and edited from *Ramtha Intensive: Soulmates* (Sovereignty, 1987), an
edited transcription of the second three-day teaching on soulmates presented by Ramtha on January 10-12, 1986. This chapter, which presents the opening address of that
Intensive, illustrates the recent nature of Ramtha's audiences and teaching style.

ally, through experience, you are going to understand the
meaning of "divine presence," the meaning of "God I Am."

Now, all of you are evolving, indeed, but *slo-w-w-w*, because you hold on to your belief systems. Know you what belief systems are? They are your illnesses, your fears, your
insecurities. They are your dogmas, your ideals, your judgments. And you hold on to them! Why? Because they give
you your identity. If you didn't have your belief system, you
think you would not know what you are. Well, these teachings
are endeavoring to break down the barriers of your belief systems so that you allow a movement of power to awaken within
you. These words really won't mean anything to you until that
power awakens. Only when you let go of your beliefs and peel
away the layers of your limited self, will you come into a state
of grace in which this knowledge will have absolute meaning
to you.

Every moment you are in this audience, I am peeling away
your limited beliefs to remove, little by little, your limited
identities. The more you learn about who you truly are, the
greater the light you will be to this plane, and the sooner you
will see Superconsciousness—an end to the dilemma of the
human drama, an end to all things that have plagued limitations upon your unlimited selves.

Now, you are here to learn about the wondrous enigma
called soulmates. I'm going to begin by telling you that
"soulmates" is a spiritual science. Know you the term
"spiritual"? You think it means something unseen, don't
you? Well, what do you call *seen*?

Everything is spiritual, because everything, even gross matter, is *volatile*; it is moving and changing.

Why do I call the understanding of soulmates a *spiritual*
science? Because this understanding transcends time, distance, and space—the things that measure scientific understandings. So, *scientifically*, there is no way to *prove* you
have a soulmate. If you apply Galileo's theory to soulmates, it
won't work. If you apply Einstein's theory to it, it won't

work. What I'm telling you is, you are *not* in a physics class!

Soulmates is a spiritual science. It is an understanding that goes *beyond* words, for if words could describe it, it would be limited knowledge, and limited knowledge does not promote *un*limited understanding.

How can one teach about something that goes beyond words, *using* practical words? He can't! I utilize words in long, lengthy processions—and in repetition—only to spark an opening within you that allows the unspeakable knowledge to come through. Know you what the unspeakable truth is? The spiritual communication is *emotion*. Emotion! Emotion is Life itself, unspoken, quiet, profound movement.

Now, for many of you this is your first audience with that which I am. I will speak to you in a moment. But there are a few of you here who have attended *many* of my audiences, who have been coming back for, perhaps, years. You think you've been studying a long time? When you sit on a rock and contemplate for seven years, *that* is a long time.

A point I wish to make about those who keep coming back to my audiences, is that I have been teaching them the same truths, over and over. Oh, I have changed my speech over the years because I found that few understood "Indeed, so-be-it, as-it-were-indeed, as-it-is-now-seen." And when I would say, "What say you, beloved entity, who has come unto this plane, as it were indeed, to spin forth a drama, as it were, separate from the kingdom from which you came?" I lost them even before I got into the second part of the sentence! *(Throws back his head and laughs uproariously)*

So with new words I kept telling the *same thing* to those who returned. Know you why? Because they weren't getting the simple message. They were *hearing* it, but they weren't *becoming* it. So I continued to manifest for them. I sent them here and there, and I made wondrous things happen in their lives. Yet all they wanted was *more*—not more of what *they* could do, but of what *I* could do for them! And it was *all* given, in love. But I still could not bring them to the understanding that they are God. I could not get them beyond that mountain because to them, it meant that if they *were* God, they had lost their identity. But know you what their identity is? One who is shrouded in limitation.

They could not get beyond that mountain because it just didn't sound right to put "God" on their driver's license. Why, they would be laughed right out of their homestead! But you see, thinking you must *say* you are God is also a limitation. You do not have to say it or wear it like an emblem! You only have to *be* it. Be!

I couldn't get them over the mountain, because they wanted to hear something different. And yet when you are God, you are *everything* different, because you have the ability to *know*. Why want all the gold in the world when it is far greater to possess the knowingness that made it *and* the world of which it is a part? Is that not greater? Of course!

All that I was telling them was *this* close *(holding up thumb and forefinger)* to an understanding. But I could not bring them to that. Opening entities' eyes to their limited beliefs and having them give them up is an arduous battle, indeed.

Now, I delivered the first teaching on soulmates to a sort of bewildered audience. They all came, hurry-scurry, thinking that the entity they might sit next to would be "The One." And I was hard-pressed in that audience to deliver knowledge that is arduous to comprehend for those who have closed minds and are only wanting a relationship.

I have contemplated that audience since then and I have come up with some *spectacular* manifestations. You're gonna get it! *(Audience laughs)*

For three days I will teach you a grand, mystical truth that no one on your plane has ever defined, because no one has ever *known* what the word "soulmate" meant. There have been speculations but never a true science of soulmates.

I'm going to teach you the science of soulmates, but I'm going to talk *around* the subject, because the science is ethereal, it is beyond words. It is a knowingness that is not within time, that is not within dimensional understanding. I will teach you this knowledge in segments, because I will teach only as long as the whole of this audience is absorbing. I will cover only those parts needed for you to receive the emotions. When the cohesive energy of this audience is at the peak of opening, you are going to be sent out and allowed to be with that emotional understanding for a moment. Understand? What I'm telling you is, I don't go by your watches!

Now, runners are very important in my audiences. They aren't entities who compete in races; they are wondrous manifestations. They are entities, thoughts, visions, experiences, and I will send you a lot of them. Why are you deserving this? Because knowledge is gained only through *experience*. And what is experience? It is an *emotional* engagement, the thought coming alive. Only through specific emotional engagements will you truly understand what I will endeavor to teach you with words.

Runners are also called "miracles of knowledge." They are not coincidental. And no matter how much you try to reason them away, they shan't go away. I will send them to you so that what I teach you will be experienced in life, the wild adventure where "god discovers God." So be it!

For many of you, this Intensive, as it is called, is going to last a *very* long time, because the knowledge I will give you, I will manifest for you until you get it—even if it takes the rest of your lifetime on this plane.

Now, know you that you are all dreamers asleep in a dream? A dreamer is one who thinks according to social consciousness and lives by its modus operandi—you know, one who does only "nice" things so as not to upset other entities, or who wants to "look good" so that everyone will think he's quite marvelous. That is living a *dream*! And it's not until you wake up from the dream that you own the wisdom of it.

What you will learn in this audience will begin to wake you up to a feeling, a knowingness of self . . . understood, finally. The runners will start to come, straightaway. There will be a *host* of them, and they shall be as unique as each of you are.

For three days you are going to sit here and you are going to drink a *lot* of bitter water. And you're going to learn greatly from what is *not* said, because you are going to *feel*. And you will sit in your little territories, called your chairs, or your spot on this carpet, and you're going to absorb. I'm not going to make you "Om" or meditate or burn incense. I will simply give unto you *knowledge*, for only knowledge allows you to transcend time and go into greater dimensions of life; to understand and embrace God, which is all things; and to live as a light to mankind.

Now, all of you have adorned yourselves to come to this audience. I am pleased. But do you know what I see when I look at you? Imagine one who has wandered into the wilderness, has fallen into a forsaken and wretched swamp, and he has become *covered* with *leeches*! Know you what a leech is? If you don't, I'll send you one so you'll have a practical demonstration of their exact modus operandi. Well, when I look at you, it's as if you are covered with layers that are liken unto leeches. And the leeches are "not allowing." They are your limited beliefs that do not *allow* your light to shine forth.

The runners are now at hand. One of their great duties is to help peel away all that keeps you in limitation so that you can begin to *know*. When you re-listen to my words, even a fortnight from now, what you heard this day will feel differently, because the peeling away of your limited identities will have already begun.

When you leave this audience, all you will be left with are *feelings*, and new insights, and a new *love of self*. That is going to be a biggie in these teachings: love of self.

You may not get everything I'm telling you for a long time. But when you do, time will stop for you. You will cease aging and you will never be diseased again. And lo, you will have vision that will penetrate and go beyond the three-dimensional plane. It will take a long time or a short time, depending upon how quickly you peel away your limitations to allow your light to come forward.

Now, there are times you will curse me. That is all right; I will still be the wind and I will still love you, in spite of your curses—because I do not *care* what you think of me. I am a grand master, and that which I am, I *am*, forever and ever and ever. So what you think of me with your limited minds does not matter. What *you* think of *you* does! It does not matter where I came from, what I look like, or what I said 35,000 years ago. Seeing who you are in the adventure called Self is all that is important. If you learn only the grand knowledge you came here for, and we begin to peel from you your ignorance and limited beliefs, it really doesn't matter what I am, does it? If my costume brings a few jolly laughs, that is all right also. One day you will know and see who be I, because you will know and see *yourself*. Understand?

Now, I have never been above—or below—doing *anything* to drive home a point. *(Audience laughs)* Well, it is a truth! There are those who have lost fortunes, just to bring them to an understanding. There are those who have gained *everything*, just to prove that they could do it. I will do whatever is necessary for your learning. The runners will bring you a sequential understanding through which you will come to love what you are, deeply. And there will be moments when you are wholly alone, and yet you will find that that is *wonderful*. Whatever it takes to get the feeling across, the knowledge across, it will come.

Now, soulmates. "Well, finally he's getting on with it!" *(Audience laughs)* You see, it's always very smart to set the ground rules before you delve right into the teaching.

Do all of you possess that enigma, that lover who comes in and out of your dreams, that immaculate vision of knighthood or womanhood? Indeed! All of you do! There is not *one* entity who does not possess a soulmate.

You know, there is a wondrous thing about mankind: once you tell him something *belongs* to him, there few things he won't do to get it—even though he doesn't *understand* what he is wanting! He wants it only because someone says it belongs to him. Well, that can be very advantageous to learning. It's like putting a carrot in front of the rabbit's nose.

All of you have a soulmate. For ten million years you have had one. Do you need one? Oh, absolutely! *(Toasts the audience)* To soulmates!

Now, your first runner. I am sending the lot of you a manifestation of the image of what you think the perfect man or perfect woman is. I want you to get caught up in your fantasies. Know you what a fantasy is? Of course you do! You are going to get caught up in your dream lover. So be it! *First* runner.

Do you have to have your soulmate in order to become God? You will always have that entity-essence with you, but no, you do not. Do you have to live with your soulmate in order to be happy? No. Do you need to go out and find your soulmate? No. The knowledge I will teach you these days and the runners that will come, will give you the understanding of why I answer this way.

I am going to take you back to the beginning of creation so that you understand what the science of soulmates means. It would take a lifetime to explain the process of creation, so I will give you only a very short synopsis of the eternal mystery of how it all began.* You will get the picture. If you don't, I'll send you a vision so you can see it.

Now, you think of God in many different ways. Your reality conceives of the all-wise, knowing intelligence in many forms. But in a greater understanding, God is Thought. In the beginning, before there was a beginning, there was only Thought—without light, without movement, without matter.

If I removed every star, every planet, every sun from this universe (in other words, took a vacuum cleaner and vacuumed them up), what would you see? You wouldn't see any

---

*Portions of the following material on creation have been excerpted and edited from *Ramtha Intensive: Change, The Days To Come*, Sovereignty, 1987.

thing because there wouldn't be any light. Without light, the eye cannot see; it cannot perceive movement.

Thought, which is God, does not move; it *is*. What allows movement is Light. Without Light, there is only empty space, without dimension or measure, without movement, with no beginning and no end. (Now, this is heavy stuff!)

What do you think holds up your world? You think it is empty space? No, it is Thought, the Is, the platform called forever.

There came an hour when Thought turned inward and contemplated its infiniteness; in other words, Thought thought about itself. When it did that, a realization occurred. That realization became Light. That was the birth of Knowledge.

Know you how electricity was created? By lowering Light; because if you take Light and lower it (slow its frequency), you divide it into a positive/negative fuse. That is how you get magnetic fields. Did you know that? *(Seeing blank expressions in the audience)* You *don't* know that. Well, maybe this *will* be a physics class! But the only way you get a magnetic field is by having negative and positive energy.

Light, as you know it, is made up of particums. In the particums of light, you have the positive/negative electrum that keeps it cohesive and explosive. But in its highest form, Light is *undivided* particums that contain and hold all of its potential lower units. And each Light particum is a cohesiveness of individual, expressive thought.

This light *(pointing to the chandeliers)* is a poor example of Light born of Thought. This is a *lower* electrum light. The greatest light is beyond your three-dimensional vision.

The Light created from Thought contemplating itself became Movement in your universe. It was Knowingness's first *adventure*, if you will. Of that Light, all of the gods were born. And who were they? *You* — and all entities, seen and unseen, that have ever lived through the divineness of their souls. You were born of God, of Is, when Thought contemplated itself, and the contemplation became Light, the

Movement . . . Emotion! In that moment, each of you became
a whole, a god—a particum of Light. That Light, which I call
the spirit or the god of your being, is your highest *individual*
form.

So, all of you prevailed in the beginning. You *were* "the
beginning" because *you* created time. Only when man created
and began to live by time, did time become a reality. Time is
one of the greatest illusions of all because it rules your lives,
and yet it doesn't exist in the Is.

The gods are the greatest light of all. From *their* light the
explosion of creativity occurred, because it is only from the
dynamic force of you, the particums of Light, contemplating
and creating like the Is once did, that a *lower* light form could
be created. And in the lower light form, the Z particum is contained. Heard you of the Z particum? *(Looks at the sea of puzzled faces)* Well, I have lost half my audience! The Z particum
is the breaking of Light into a lower form.

From the Light particums were created the gases that created what your scientists think was a "big bang," a large
blast—you know, when boom! everything sort of happened.
Well, you can say that, but it didn't quite happen that way;
that is only measuring time. You have to forget about time in
order to *know*.

The universe, the sun, the earth—they were not created
from an explosion. The "big bang" is only called that because your scientists don't know what happened *prior* to that.
But the gods were first. From them, the creative element en-
sued, and it has been ongoing ever since.

What did the gods create from? Thought, of course.
Thought is everlasting Life, the *forever* Is. Thought taken to
its lowest form is called *gross matter*, which is made up of
atoms. Each atom has a billion particums within it. Have I lost
you? It's called *Infinite* Mind.

The only way the gods could create from the flow of
Thought that gave them life, was to have something, termed
the soul, that could hold Thought still. Your soul is like a

computer. It holds and stores Thought. Without your soul you would know no thing, you could express no thing, you could create no thing, you would *be* no thing, except Is.

The soul records every thought you've ever had. It does not record it as a thought, but rather as what the thought electrically did to your light form; it's called feelings. Feelings are the basis of the gaseous matter of your universe; feelings *created* gaseous matter.

What gives substance to the atoms is called the Z particum. That was the first feeling *manifested*, and it gave life to the whole of your universe. Creation began from the Z particum dividing into the X and Y particums to create *combustion*, gases, that which is called your suns. From the suns, gross matter was born. The suns lowered the electrum to create matter, particles of which scattered for endless time. And all along, space, the quiet, the void called Thought, allowed Light to play upon it. So, matter was born, but the gods, the Light particums, still prevailed.

The suns gave birth to the planets by an explosion of *powerful* energy, which rotated around the suns in an explosive fission. As this energy rotated and moved into an orbit further away from the sun, it began to cool. As it rotated, and the more it cooled, the more hollow the planets became on the inside, because the rotation and centrifugal force thrust everything that was in the center toward the outermost perimeter.

Gods created the first livable planet in your solar system. It was called Melina, and it was the first planet birthed from your sun. It was created from light giving birth to mass, a natural process. There the gods played, creating light forms. (At this point, you are each still one god, *undivided*; you are without gender, as it were.) When, through their competitive spirit, the gods destroyed Melina (remnants of it now circle Saturn), many of them went to the far reaches of your solar system, where they still are this day. Others went to the planet that is in line with your Earth but on the other side of the sun, a planet that your scientists will discover before the end of this century. (So there is another planet out there that you didn't know you had.)

After Melina was destroyed and other planets had been created, your Earth evolved from the side of your mother sun and was set into orbit. Through its rotation, it cooled. In time (we are talking of billions and billions of years, where there really is no time), it was impregnated and ready for life. Only after your planet became hollow on the inside and cooled on the surface did gods begin to make their homes here and to create, in the embryo state, *all* cellular mass.

Now, have you ever seen the planet Venus? It is covered in clouds, is it not? Why do you think the clouds are there? They are oceans in the stratum, which will one day be the oceans upon that planet. Life is coming to be on the surface of that planet through water, aqueous substance. It is a paradise there. The temperature is constant because the cloud cover is a conduit for light. It takes the light from the sun and disperses it evenly around that planet. Thus the whole of that planet is like a warm womb in which new life-forms are developing, just like it happened here. It is a reaction and another play, another drama happening.

So your Earth evolved. In time, a cloud cover surrounded it, just like the one that now surrounds Venus. Soon, life here came to a three-dimensional, aqueous substance level. So now we have come from light to water. And the gods, through their desire, through their souls, created every life-form upon your Earth. And *you* did it all.

Now, this has been sort of a short re-cap of eternity, correct? *(Picks up his glass and toasts the audience)* To creation! May you know it all!

Think about this for a moment: Have you ever watched an exotic hummingbird gathering nectar from a lily? If you haven't, I'll send you one. So be it! Have you ever watched the metamorphosis of a worm into a splendidly-arrayed butterfly? Have you ever seen the pearl hue of a fish in a babbling brook at midday? If you haven't, I'll send you to where you can see one.

Have you ever counted how many species of insects there are? Have you ever counted the species of the animal kingdom? How many kinds of flowers are there? Who do you think created those things?

Who taught the great heron how to catch fish by scaring them and running them to the shore, where he would shade his eyes with his wing so he could see them in the water? Who gave him the intelligence to do that?

Who created the flower that smells like rotting meat, even *looks* like rotting flesh? Who designed it so it would attract a fly to go in and lay its eggs inside the flower to create maggots, which would be digested by the flower?

Who created the grand plant that grows a leaf so broad, it wraps around itself to collect the morning dew, drop by precious drop, so that a very special little frog can live there and keep it company? Who gave it that knowledge?

Which one of you clever entities taught the salmon how to live and frolic in a far, far sea? And when their lives were spent and their souls were heavy with experience, who taught them how to bring forth a new generation so that they themselves could come back as their own young and feed off the rotting flesh of their former bodies? Who taught them how to do that? Hmm?

Which one of you women taught a gazelle how to run like a little dancer, seemingly born of wings? Who taught her how to give birth to her babe? Who whispered in the babe's ear to stay still like a stone? And who gave the babe the knowingness to emit no smell?

These are only a few of the wonders of this life, but know you who created all of these things? *You* did. Know you *how* you did it? By feeling from the Is and capturing that emotion within your souls. You felt everything into life. You breathed life into those creative, aqueous forms called cells. You gave the cells a *pattern*.

Did you know that each cell possesses the pattern of the

whole? Did you know that from a scraping of tissue from your nose, your scientists can clone your double? It's true.

You breathed life into what you created by feeling it into existence. This "breath" was not so it could be a breathing creature. The breath of life was instincts, called "patterns of destiny." You gave your creations their intelligence, which would go on and on and on. Sounds absurd? Well, there is far more to the story. I will send you runners of vision, and they will fill in the blanks where no words come. So be it!

Now, did you know that thought can pass through matter? Well, you have visions of spiritual entities and ghosts who pass through walls, right? They *do*, because they are vibrating at a higher frequency than mass, the three-dimensional frequency. Mass is coagulated thought, but a thought can pass through it.

What did this mean to you, who were Thought in the form of Light? It meant that although you had breathed the patterns of destiny into your creations, into the *whole* of this world, you couldn't smell the rose you created or touch that furry little creature called an otter. You couldn't cuddle, smell, taste, hear, see. The only way you could be a part of this thriving kingdom was to lower your light frequency and condense *yourself* into mass. That is when you really got into trouble!

The gods created and inhabited bodies so that they could experience the kingdom they created here. And I must tell you, if we brought forward one of those bodies this day, you would be horrified, because it wasn't what you would call beautiful. But it was a wondrous vehicle that allowed the gods to go in and out of this kingdom.

Now, in the beginning of the experiments with man, bodies were sort of like a wardrobe: you had a selection of them, but they were without gender. And it was very easy for a god to create a body. All he had to do was envision it and *feel* it, and it became! That's how you manifest everything.

There came an hour when the gods desired to inhabit bodies that reflected the uniqueness of each god. So they contemplated, as the Is once did, and they came up with the idea of creating male *and* female bodies that could copulate to bring forth the species called human. The only problem was, no god wanted to become either male *or* female! So they conceived of becoming *both*—by lowering and splitting themselves. That meant that each god would lower its light and soul, lower them from the pinnacle of Light to the lower electrums where *division* occurs—because if you take this grand light and slow its frequency, it soon splits to become positive/negative.

So each god lowered its light. When it became positive/negative, the light and the soul both split. And the god would stay split as long as it chose to remain in a lower frequency.

Whew! Got through that one! Creation is always a toughie! *(Toasts the audience)* To the split!

Now, a whole mass of gods each created two bodies through cellular design, one to house the positive charge and one to house the negative charge. The negative would be called the female gender, the positive would be called the male gender. Hormones would flow in the body according to the electrical charge housed in it.

In the female, the doors (the chakras, or seals) were set. When the female energy, the negative energy, entered a body designed to house that energy, the locks turned, all seven seals opened up, the flow of "hormone balance" began, and behold! the female was born. Into the male, who also had the seven doors, the positive energy entered. The hormones began to flow, and behold! the masculine entity was born. Remember, we are talking of one god splitting and becoming a pair of bodies: positive *and* negative.

The penis, the breasts, the vagina—these did not exist in the cellular mass of the body at the moment of the split. It was the hormones' control, their *harmony*, that would bring these things into being.

So, the negative charge entered the female body. As the body was in slumber, the breasts grew and the body softened and took form, because the seven ductless glands were now open and secreting hormones—*harmony*. The soul-spirit split was in harmony with that body. The positive charge entered the "clay" of the male body, turned the locks of the seven doors, and the body began to grow into masculine form.

So awaken from slumber, man!... awaken from slumber, woman!—soulmates, looking into one another's eyes, *seeing* Self for the first time ever! seeing the reflection, the energy! feeling both of their souls and spirits sharing the same experience, except in a different version. Are you beginning to see? Are the lights turning on? *(Picks up his glass and toasts the audience)* To Life!

Now, contemplate for a moment the science of genetics. Think about what makes genetic memory.

Each of you possesses, in your loins and in your womb, seeds that contain the genetic memory that can create another entity. What do you think creates the individual chromosomes that carry genetic memory? Well, what created *everything*? Feelings! Genetic memory is created through *emotion*.

Ten million years ago on your plane the gods split to become male and female energies. And every adventure they had in matter brought forth emotion. Every moment they felt something of high emotion, the chromosome structures inside the sperm and egg received an imprint. *That* is what is creating your body, right this moment. That is the science the gods devised to create new bodies with new characteristics, which would be different rather than being clones.

So, soulmates are "born." They copulate. But before copulation, the man is running from a predator. As he runs, he is desiring with great emotion for his legs to be longer and swifter. In that moment, he creates a new pattern on his chromosome structure, through *desire*. So, the chromosomes are changed. He runs back to his hovel to find his mate, who during the day had been joyful in spirit; so, in her chromosomes there is the imprint "happy life." They copulate and a physical body is conceived, one which will have, genetically, happy cells and longer legs!

Other gods, now splitting, start choosing their bodies from the *offspring* of soulmates. The positive energy from the split chooses a body with a positive charge. When he comes in, it is a new adventure of touch and smell, of suckling for the first time at his mother's breast, of being carried on his father's shoulder and getting a spectacular view of a meadow. When he grows to full height he will have long limbs and he will out-run his father. And his father will say, "You are, indeed, the son of my desire." You see how it works?

What evolved you genetically? What caused evolution? What caused the ongoingness? What caused your skin to get finer and your head to get bigger? *Feelings*. Because every moment, your emotions are manifesting. And guess what is recording them all? Your immortal soul.

For ten million years you have lived on this plane and you have evolved through emotions.

Now, soulmates *shared* the paradise of life here, because each was receiving from the other the greatest gift of all: feelings. The joy of the woman birthing the child—that *feeling* was given to her soulmate, the other part of herself. What wondrous "psychic" experience was going on here? They were the *same* soul, *same* spirit, and whatever one experienced the other felt.

The next lifetime, they chose, perhaps, to be in bodies dwelling in different lands from one another, because those are the bodies they picked for their next adventure into life.

Where is *your* soulmate right now? For most of you, your soulmates are on this plane at this moment. For others, your soulmates are on another plane at this moment, or in another universe at this moment. Know you what connects you together? Feelings. You are always this close. *This close*!

So the one god split and became two individuals, soulmates; yet it still remained whole, one god. Their thoughts, which manifest as feelings, flow between them. You are attached to your soulmate liken unto some divine elastic cord. It can stretch into forever, and yet it always remains intact.

You're as close to your soulmate as a breath away, a moment away, a passion away, because, remember: time, distance and space do not measure the unseen, do not measure the Isness, called God.

You and your soulmate experience, you learn, you *share*. What your soulmate has experienced, *you* have experienced, and vice versa, because you share knowingness, you share understanding with each other.

You and your soulmate are connected for all time. When we look at your past, we consider two entities, not one. The two of you are one god on an amazing journey. You are one god expressing as both man *and* woman. And for ten million years the two of you have been experiencing this plane, together.

***

12

The Prize
Of Creation

Who created the universes that you have not now the eyes to see? Who set the stars into the heavens with a backdrop called forever? Who created the change in the leaves, in the seasons? Who created the flower and the enigma called man? Who did all these wondrous things? You! Why? To feel. To understand.

Everything you have ever done, that you have ever created, from the time you were born of your beloved Father, has been for the purpose of feelings, emotion. Everything! There is not *one thing* you do that does not equate feelings to you.

Each of you is a powerful, emotional entity who has the ability to feel. Without feeling, you are not! Feeling is the creator and the prize of life; it always has been and it always shall be.

Look at you! You look, act, and dress certain ways because doing that makes you *feel* certain ways. You do everything, not for the sake of doing it, but for the feelings derived from it—a treasure which cannot be seen. You see the body, the instrument that makes it possible to experience feelings, but you never see the grandest reality of your life.

The *only* reason the body was created was so that you could have a vehicle to experience a feeling sensation from the three-dimensional reality. You, the creators of the flower, inhabited a body so you could embrace the flower. In your embracing it, it mirrored back "self," the god within you: "This I created, and from this splendid ideal I shall create more and more and more. And I shall *feel* my creations, for feeling is the *prize* of creation." It certainly is. For a god does not *know* it is a living thing until it creates "itself," and that which it creates mirrors back to itself its power and creative genius.

Once you had touched the flowers, seen the animals, felt the wind, lain on the sand, what was the next creation? More! And so were born tools, transports, societies, religions, kingdoms, histories... for the god within you is a *compulsive* creator.

As you continued to create in matter, you were *driven* to experience all of the creations here so you could derive the treasure of their reality in feelings. As life on this plane became an ongoing creative principle, you became so focused in your creations and so identified with your body, that you soon forgot the divine fire within you, and you became entrapped in the bodily experience.

From the time you forgot who you are, your quest has been to find yourself again, through beliefs in heaven and burning fires of hell; through love, religion, dissension, and war—through *anything* by which you might realize your god power and the foreverness of your life.

Creator, you have created your sorrow. You have created your depression and your anger. You have created your misery, hurt, and despair. And you have created your happiness and joy. You have created *every moment* of your life, and from each creation, you obtain feelings that allow you to better understand the fire that lives within you, called, if you will, God Almighty.

Now that all things have been created, what is the last frontier of creative value? *You*—the creator of this illusion. Now your drive is not to create; it is to understand the greatest mystery of all times—you!

Why are you the greatest mystery? Because your greatest desire is the desire to know and understand self—your worth, your power, why you do what you do, and how you relate to all other entities. And this life allows you to have emotional interactions with other entities through which you can gain that understanding. That is why you have chosen your family, friends, and labors. That is why you love, marry, and have your relationships. You are choosing to interact with certain entities in order to understand yourself, seen through their reflection; for whatever you perceive in another will represent you to yourself every moment. If you see another as horrible, ugly, despicable, it is only because you think that *you* are that. If you see beauty, kindness, compassion in another, it is only because *you* possess that. You never really understand yourself until you put mirrors in front of you who reflect all aspects of yourself—your ideals, your fears, your judgments of self, and how you are expressing in life.

Why is love so important to you? It is a wild, free-moving feeling that allows you to see who you are and to be profoundly moved by the *great* entity that you are. And whenever love is felt, it reminds you of the joy of being free and unlimited within your being.

Now, you never truly love another entity. You never can, because you can never *know* the other entity. You love the other only for what they express that you identify with. They mirror back to you "self," seen openly within them. When you see in another all the things you love in yourself, you become "in love."

Love is identity, love is feeling. Loving another allows you to experience myriad feelings, from jealousy, doubt, anger, and hurt, to passion, joy, and ecstasy. The interaction of self with self brings out the full spectrum of feelings that allows you to identify all aspects of yourself, seen through an emotional understanding.

Love for another is the love of self. When lovers embrace they do not feel the other, they feel self. When they are emotional with one another they are being emotional with self. God, in his wonderful love affair with self, is seen through the mirror of another. Deep and profound and magical love occurs when another blooms with the very essence you are within your being. That is why all love so intently.

Now, why have you returned to this plane? To complete your identity as God. That is simply the way it is. You did not come back here to be a great conqueror or healer. You did not return to be a minister or a politician (you have enough of them!). Your destiny was not ordained eons ago, for eons ago you had no conception of this moment. You came back to this level of life simply to fulfill emotional lackings within you. That is why you do every thing you do—because you are *driven* to experience it for an feeling knowingness within your soul. What does this add to the character called "you"? It means you need never experience that again, for wisdom now says, "I have experienced myself in another reality of feelings. I now understand and I am complete with that emotion." And when your soul, the greatest scribe of all, closes its books—for no more emotional understanding can be obtained from *this* plane, and you know who and what you are—you go on to another adventure. And that adventure is *wherever* you wish to create it.

The reason for all creation has been feelings, emotion. Everything has been created for that sublime purpose. And the prize of all created values is called "completion."

To manifest *all* you desire in order to complete yourself in this life, speak forth your desires from the lord-god of your being. When you do, you are speaking from your lord-soul/god-light—the totality of your isness—as an aligned unit. When you speak from the lord-god of your being, *anything* you desire you will have.

The secret to manifesting your desires is: Whatever you want, become it *totally* in feelings. *Feel* your desire. *Become* the desire within your being. Become the feeling so that the emotion exalts the totality of your being—so that you utterly *are* the thing you have desired. Do not simply visualize the image of what you want. Whatever you want, *feel* what it would feel like if you had it. Then the Father, the platform of Life, will manifest into your life whatever object or situation that will bring to you the *same* feeling. That is how you become a magician. That is how you create your destiny. That is, indeed, how you complete whatever feeling is needed within your soul.

All of you are still beggars! You continuously fight the wills of others to have what you desire. You beg for the pence that buys you bread. You labor in the most pitiful ways to obtain food to feed the body so that it may continue to have the capacity to feel. Stop being beggars. Cease it! Speak from the lord-god of your being and *feel* what you want. Feel it, until you *become* what you wish within your being. The outward, material, lowest plane of all will manifest it to add to your material kingdom, so that the emotion gained from it will match the emotion of the "kingdom within," which will live on into eternity.

Now, Yeshua ben Joseph, whom you call Jesus of Nazareth, taught that the kingdom of heaven is within you, yet few have ever known what he meant. The kingdom of heaven is *indeed* within you, because you have the ability to possess *anything* in the kingdom of God simply by becoming it in feelings. What does a rich man feel like? How would it feel to have palaces untold? Fame? In your kingdom you can have all of those things by feeling them to the ultimate within you, and then drawing them to you. And soon, you will tire of the illusion of matter, because you will have come to realize that you don't *need* it. You will realize that you can experience *every feeling* that could ever be derived from matter, right *within you*. That is why Yeshua said that his kingdom was no longer of this world. He realized that he no longer needed the illusion of mass to create feelings within his being; he could create the emotions derived from matter right wherever he was, in the quietness of his own thought processes.

The true treasure of this plane is not the kingdoms created here; it is the feelings derived from them. That is the only thing you take with you when you leave this plane. And if your emotions are those of limited thoughts—guilt, sorrow, hate, fear, insecurity—when you die, you will have to come back here, for emotion determines each next adventure. That is why I say unto you, "Do everything for the sake of joy." When you live wholly for the sake of joy within you, you are living in the grandest heaven. And that joy you *will* take with you. Your material kingdom will be left to others, who will eagerly grab up its mute testimony to your ingeniousness.

Self's greatest knowingness is when self realizes that is an imageless, faceless, awesome, ongoing power that need do *nothing* but be. When self *knows* it is God, the Is, it can be whatever it wishes, at whatever moment it desires to be it.

You have the power within you to raise your bodily vibrations and to take your body wherever your thought wishes to go. When you can take your thought to be the laughter of a child in five hundred years to come, that is when you know you are God. That knowingness can be had *now*, for it lies within your feelings. To realize your godhood, you must remove all the images you think you must be, and become the isness of God, which is the totality of feelings. To know the Father within you, you must allow yourself to *feel* and to express *all* your emotions.

You don't know what you truly look like, but you are a great ball of light, so brilliant in its core that the color is uncertain. The corona outside of the fireball is the greatest rose color you have ever seen. From the corona, the rays that extend outward are golden rods of light. So awesome is the power of your light that it has the ability to take thought and create with an emotion whatever it pleases.

• Why is it important to love what you are? Because in loving yourself, you bring into harmony and perfect alignment "you"—your kingdom, your power, your ability to manifest. Never, ever, *not* love you! Love the fire that is within you, for that fire created the rose, the bird, the stars in your heavens, and the universes within and without. Love life, for without it, dearest masters, you can experience none of your creations. Without life, you cannot have little playhouses to arrange, become depressed over, oppressed over, worried over, happy over, miserable over in your little games. Without life and the toys that are here, you would not be able to feel—the greatest treasure of all, the greatest reality of all.

This life is an illusion, a game, an imaginative adventure to gain the reality called Self. The more you experience and love who you are, the greater you will understand joy and the mystery of self.

You are not a man or a woman. You are *God*, a *great* entity who is playing a game to experience a feeling. And when you are complete with this heaven, you will fulfill yourself, get upon the back of the wind, and be off to yet a grander heaven. Simply!

***

13

The Quaking Silence

Master: I have several questions for you. First, I've felt such a connection to you ever since I first heard the name Ramtha. Could you tell me what our relationship is?

Ramtha: Love, master. I *love* you. That is our relationship. And you are *worth* that.

Master: Thank you. I felt that the moment I met you.

Ramtha, speaking about love, I feel that I need to be released from my ego so that I can love more fully. Can you help me to become egoless?

Ramtha: Master, you can *never* be egoless, for ego is your identity; it is who you are, which is indeed God. Now, *altered* ego means altered God, altered identity, limited identity. Altered ego is the limited thought that sees yourself as less than what you truly are within the core of your being.

Never desire to be without your ego. Desire instead to remove from your thinking the judgment of self that alters the understanding that you are a god, an isness. When you stop judging yourself, you allow the awareness of your godhood to come forth. Then your ego-identity will not be singular, limited man, but the unlimited totality of ongoing Life. Then you can't *help* but love everything and every entity, for when you do, you are loving self and God, which are now known to be one and the same.

Master: You make it sound so simple.

Ramtha: It *is* simple, master. And the simpler you see it, the simpler it becomes.

Master: I also have several questions about prayer. First, I want to know *who* I'm supposed to pray to. When I was younger, I was taught to pray to Jesus by saying, "Lord Jesus Christ, have mercy on me, for I am a sinner." But I'm not sure if I should pray to God or to Jesus.

Ramtha: Who do you pray to? Entity, when you pray, you pray to God, the Father, the Source. You do not pray to anyone *but* the Source! And where do you go to do that? You pray *within* yourself. Self *is* the divine temple of God. There is no temple of stone or wood that is greater than "the garden within." To pray to the Father, you go within yourself, wherever you are, and commune with that power within, the peace within, the essence of love that is all that you are. Do that for however long it is necessary for the whole of that feeling to reach every fiber of your being. That will give you the strength to face the world with love, peace, and joy in your being.

Now, master, I wish for you to understand this about prayer: It was originally created simply as a way to remain aligned with the god within you, the feelings within. It was created as a way to turn aside for a few moments from the illusions of matter and, in the quiet of one's being, contemplate what one desired, and call it forth into a manifested experience. But for many on your plane, prayer has become a mindless, ritualistic act practiced according to *dogma*. And dogma says you must utter prayer from the understanding that you are an imperfect, wretched, powerless little entity who must beg and plead with someone outside of yourself to fulfill your desires, approve of you, forgive you, save you, love you, give you life forever and ever. A sure sign of the ineffectiveness of *that* kind of prayer is that so many of your churchyards sit next to graveyards.

Those who pray to *another* for mercy will *never* have it. No one but *self* has the power to forgive self. You are the only one who can offend yourself, you are the only one who truly judges yourself, and you are the only one who can show mercy and compassion toward yourself.

Within you, master, lies the power to create universes. Within you lies the power to manifest whatever dream you fancy, for the whole of your reality was created from dreams. And within *you*, blessed entity, also lies the power to give your power away through dogmas and rituals that convince you that you are wretched, and that your life is not wholly in your own hands.

Cease rituals. Cease following dogmas. Cease them! Cease routines. Trust the god within to speak to you, guide you, remind and teach you. Every time you do anything *given* to you as a way to life, or truth, or happiness, you are putting your power and your life into the hands of others; you are putting your trust in another's belief, not in self—the accepter of laws, thus the ultimate giver of them. You are giving credence to the thought that your god, your guide, your good is not always within *you*.

Never utter from your mouth any words that say you are not *already* what you want to be, for whatever you say is an open command to your soul to manifest it into your days to come. Speak and act as if you are your ideal *now*, *this moment*. Then, one moment later, one wondrous now in your future, so it will be. If you say, "Forgive me," so will you always need to be forgiven. If you say, "I am a sinner," so will you always be. Do you understand?

Master: I think so. But I stopped saying that prayer a long time ago. I was just using it as an example.

Ramtha: Indeed? Well, think about the things in your life that you do ritually, not because you *desire* to do these things, but because you think that if you don't do them, you will not be accepted or loved. Religions, master, are not the only keepers of dogma, rituals, standards, and the like. Think about every word that flows from your mouth, and what you are saying. Now, what else desire you?

Master: Ramtha, is it true that through prayer we have the power to heal someone who is diseased?

Ramtha: Indeed, but only if the entity accepts the thoughts and the love you are sending forth.

Master: Then, I would like to understand how to pray for someone else.

Ramtha: What prayer truly is, is taking a moment to bend your mind toward an object or an entity, and speaking forth what you want. It is taking a moment to align your energies in a particular direction and telling the Source, "This is what I wish. So be it!" And whatever you pray for is easily rendered when there are no other wills involved. If there are, the manifestation can come into being only when all wills associated with that manifestation are in alignment.

Master: But *how* does prayer works? Is it the repetition? I've noticed that at times when I have become very frustrated and have yelled out what I wanted, it brought amazing and instantaneous results.

Ramtha: I dare say it does!

Master: But what makes it work?

Ramtha: It is not repetition, master. It is the *emotion* that manifests. You can repeat something, over and over and over again, but unless you *feel* what you are saying and take it to heart, it will not occur.

Everyone manifests their desires by *feeling* the desire—by embracing the thought into emotion. And the more intense the feeling, the quicker the manifestation. That is why in your fits of emotion, when you have bolted forth what you wanted in a demanding tone, it happened quickly. That should have told you everything!

Now, master, when you pray for someone else, who are you to say what is good for that entity, when all things have their purpose for being? To want another to be healed does a great injustice to the entity, for he has created his illness as a direct result of his emotional structure.

Never pray for an entity's sickness to be removed. *Love* him. Know that his will has created this, and have the grace and the mercy to allow him to do with his life whatever he needs to. What an entrapment it is for the entity lying sick within the infirmary, fighting for its life only because others are praying for the soul of the entity to hold on to its pain-ridden body, when really it has found "the peace that passeth all understanding," and it wants to go there. It is better to say to the entity, "Bless you. May your will be done," for that encourages the soul of its being to enact its wisdom in creating whatever the entity needs to experience. The deepest love for another is when you leave the entity alone and give him the grace to do whatever is necessary for its learning and its happiness. You understand?

Master: I think so. Can I ask you one last question?

Ramtha: Indeed.

Master: You said earlier that prayer was created as a way to keep in touch with the god within us and to manifest all the things we desire. Is there a prayer you can give me to say, one that will help do that?

Ramtha: Beautiful entity, your *daily life* is a prayer! How you *live* it this day is how it will be, for your tomorrows are created by all of your thoughts, feelings, and actions this very day. For you to become centered and speak forth a prayer, telling the Father that you desire this or that, is all well and good. But if you desire for something to be, and yet in the next moment you live as though it will *not* be, you are living a duality, a parallel truth, and *that* will manifest. One's actions speak truth the loudest. You see?

Master: Yes. But I feel it would help me if I could recite something to myself each day. Actually, I had in mind a particular prayer that you recited at an audience that a friend of mine attended several months ago. My friend thought it was a very beautiful prayer, but he failed to write it down. So, I want to know if you would recite it again.

Ramtha: Can you not create a prayer as beautifully?

Master: In my own style, yes, I can.

Ramtha: Would your style be different from that of the lover of your being, or the entity sitting next to you?

Master: Yes.

Ramtha: If I give a prayer to everyone, they will repeat what *I* have spoken, not what *they* have created of their own emotion. You understand? This does not mean that I am ornery and do not wish to comply. It means I am wise.

(After pause) Entity, do this: Every day, speak to the lord-god that lives within you, the quaking silence that is the reason you are, and exalt the divine quality of yourself. Simply say to yourself, "How *beautiful* I am. I am awed by that which I am, for I am powerful, creative, and the reason for all life. I am forever the light and the love of God." That is all you need do.

No one can lift self, love self, as self can. The grandest compliment self can be paid is by its own wondrous being. That is why every day, everyone should lift themselves to such a lofty perception.

Exalt yourself at all times, quietly, within self. And love your body, tenderly and dearly, for it is your vehicle to experience this plane. It is the channel of kingdoms to come. It is the home of God. *Everyone* needs to do that. Everyone needs to look at their hands, their skin, their feet, their face—every part of them—and caress it.

So, caress yourself, master, and every day of your existence, *love* who you are. That is enacting the greatest prayer of all. Do you understand?

Master: Yes.

Ramtha: Just *be*, master, and trust your god to fulfill all of your dreams and desires. And when wonderful things occur, appreciate them, and bless the Father within you. You *deserve* them.

Master: Thank you. And I also want to thank you for the many blessings I've received from you.

Ramtha: Indeed! Master, you haven't needed to even utter a prayer to have them occur. Ever wonder why?

Master: No. I just accept.

Ramtha: Ah, master, that is a *wondrous* way to be! Apply it

in every other aspect of your life, and the kingdom of heaven
is yours. So be it.

***

14

Hold Them In Your Arms

Ramtha: Master, what say you?

Master: I would like you to bless my hands so that I can use them to heal people who are in pain, who are suffering and so unhappy in life. I also want to heal children who are born victims of birth defects or mental retardation.

Ramtha: Most noble request, master. But tell me, do you believe everyone is equal?

Master: Yes.

Ramtha: What think you equality is?

Master: Equality is knowing that everybody is the same, that they're all gods.

Ramtha: Indeed. For each possesses the same will to create with thought whatever they choose. Do you believe that you can heal someone against his will?

Master: I don't believe anything can be done to someone against his will.

Ramtha: That is, indeed, a correct statement. That is why there are no victims in life.

Entities born into bodies that are diseased or deformed or lacking in the realms of what you term "normal" are not victims, master. For the entity entering the body is not ignorant of the conditions he is inhabiting.

Each entity chooses his embodiment and designs it according to what he wants it to be. That is his divine right. He is the one who has dominion over that which is forming within the womb. The soul is placed within the union of the seed and the egg upon conception, but the spirit, which is the caretaker of the soul, may reject the body at any time it is forming. The spirit may even wait up to 12 months after the birth of the body before it takes hold of it. If the formation of the body within the womb is not according to the will of the entity who shall be the controller in that embodiment, the spirit of its being will recall the soul from the body and allow the body to die. You call that nature, but in truth, that is free will.

What of those entities who are born, nonetheless, with bodily impairments? They have simply chosen to be this way. They have allowed this to occur because they want to experience this.

Master: Ramtha, it bothers me to hear you say that. Why would someone *want* to be born crippled or retarded? That's really hard for me to understand.

Ramtha: Master, the reasons are many, but in simplicity, they are always because the entity *wants* to be that way for the experiences he is desiring—because it makes him happy.

Many choose impaired embodiments precisely because their happiness is to express on this plane without the function of physical beauty—for perhaps they are ready to understand and appreciate the greater beauty that lies behind the illusion of the flesh. They can simply be who they are without worrying about being accepted for their appearance or physical ability or grand intellect, whatever is esteemed here. When an entity has that burden taken from him, he can more readily experience true joy and a profound love for self in that life; and when he passes this plane, he is beauteous in his light and happy in his soul.

When you leave this plane, master, you go to a graduated understanding where you are thought and emotion, not mass. There, you are bodiless in regard to a molecular form, but you are full-bodied in a light spectrum. There, the beauty or acceptability of the body is not measured. ♦

The physical body is only an instrument to gain emotional experiences in mass and to fulfill certain needs for the prize of life, called wisdom. If an entity chooses a malformed embodiment, that body is in a condition of perfection for the entity inhabiting it. It is perfect for him to gain the experiences he is desiring, and he *wants* it that way. For perhaps only in that way can he learn to appreciate the body, or to humble himself enough to understand those who are the same as he.

Master, if it takes doing away with a part of your body for you to learn to love yourself, or to experience pure joy, or to learn to have compassion and love for *everyone*, then *let it be done*.

Now, these simpletons that you speak of, master, are very much aware of their lives. Although they may not have a great capacity for intellectual expression, they have the same capacity for thought and emotion that all do. Intellect never determined intelligence; it never determined a god.

Many of these entities are *great* masters, for they do not judge others, and they love all people, regardless of how they look or how they express. They also do not worry, they forgive continuously, and they are indeed happy. If it hurts you to look upon them, perhaps you should reassess your values.

What of the little bodies that have been cast aside, their bellies bloated terribly, their bones protruding through thin skin? You say to me, "How could they be happy? Why would they choose to suffer like this?"

Beloved woman, there is an ideal on this plane of what happiness is supposed to look like. I will argue the ideal, and I will win. Happiness is not only a jolly little entity with wings on its back who sits upon puffy clouds singing wonderful songs. It is whatever experience an entity creates to bring *fulfillment* to his being. And who are you to determine what fulfillment is for another entity?

Many choose to be born into wretched conditions for the challenge of rising above such conditions. Or they desire to come back to help and to teach entities experiencing that, for they have a kinship with those entities. Many do so to gain compassion for others, or a greater love for themselves and the desire to choose a better existence in their life to come. The reasons are many, and they are unique to each entity.

No one is *ever* born a victim of fate or circumstance. Entities born directly into sickness, impairment in their bodies, or wretched conditions, have chosen that for themselves, fully knowing the conditions they will face. They have chosen their bodies and their parents for their own reasons, all of which equates to *want*, which equates to *happiness*. Understand?

Master: I think so. *(Thinks for a moment)* Well, is there something I can do for people who become ill or diseased *after* they come into this life?

Ramtha: Master, wanting to heal others is very admirable. It shows much love on your part. But you can never heal anyone else. The true healer is the one needing to be healed. Healing is accomplished through the attitude of the one who is diseased, for the attitude created the disease in the first place.

The body is a wondrous machine, if you will, that is *wholly* a product of the thought processes of the one who inhabits it. Every moment, it paints the clearest, most intimate portrait of all of one's feeling-attitudes. Every thought an entity has registers as an emotion within its soul, and that emotion sends to every cell within the body an electrical spark that feeds each cell. Love, freedom of expression, appreciation of unseen beauty, patience, living in the moment, allowing life to be—these are all attitudes that spark health and foreverness within the cells of the body. Self-hate, self-denial, feelings of unworthiness, insecurity, jealousy, guilt, anger, failure, sorrow—these attitudes degenerate the cells within the body to create illness and diseases, for they are attitudes that alter life, that inhibit it. When your attitudes do not permit your life to be lived in freedom and in ease, the body will eventually mirror your attitudes and become dis-eased.

The body will always reflect and represent an entity's collective thinking. Those who hate themselves and despise their own bodies will often cause madness in their cells, called cancer, which will devour their embodiments. Those who are selfish will often manifest the illness termed diabetes. Those who cannot express their love will often manifest diseases of the heart. Those who have deep guilt and remorse, feeling that they must be punished and must suffer, will often manifest diseases that create great agony in their beings.

Now, everyone possesses genetic patterns within the cells of their bodies that predispose their bodies to certain diseases. Your body is prone to the same diseases your parents manifested, for their collective attitudes were programmed into the genetic matter of the egg and sperm that came together to form the body you inhabited. That is how disease is inherited in the body. But these "chromosome patterns," as they are called, do not become activated unless you adopt the *same* attitudes that prevailed within your lineage. If you do, the chromosome structures within the DNA automatically begin to release these patterns into the body to create like diseasements. It is all very scientific and all very true.

Attitude is the cure. That is what heals. When one begins to love himself and remove from his thought processes the attitudes that inhibit life, then peace and harmony will begin to reign within the cellular structures. But the entity must first *want* to be healed. Want is the key. That is the manifesting power. No one can lift illness from an entity until the entity wishes for it to be lifted and chooses to use another as a tool for healing. Many are not ready to let go of their sickness—even though they say they want to be well—for in their souls, they are not complete with the purpose it is serving. Many will remain ill their entire life no matter what a physician or a master does for them, because the illness affords them attention, and they are afraid of losing the attention; so they will not allow the illness to be removed.

• The only healer of illness or disease is the creator of it, which is self. Nothing can heal the body unless it first heals the attitude. Do you understand?

Master: Yes.

Ramtha: The healer, master, is desire, acceptance, and love of self.

Master: Ramtha, let's say that someone truly *wants* to be healed. Is there something I can do to help that healing occur?

Ramtha: Indeed, master. You can bring forth *love*—the greatest healer of all. I help to heal entities by loving them, by seeing them as perfect, regardless of who they are or how they are expressing. They relax in their beings and allow the hormones that are locked up in great glands to flow into the body, and the body begins to heal.

The greatest, most noble works you could ever accomplish will be achieved through love. Love is the mover, entity, and it can redesign anything.

Look into the eyes of the entity and love him, profoundly. When you can love a leper and hold him in your arms—even though he will not look upon your face, for he is shameful of his ugliness and stench—if you can hold him in his desperation and *love* him, and see him in perfection, that is what heals. He will look into your eyes and see no judgment there, only love and life. Soon, he will tell the soul of his being that perhaps he is not what he has feared himself to be—that in reality he is as this wondrous entity has seen him. When an entity knows he is loved and held in esteem by another, he lifts himself to become that ideal.

If you desire to be a healing influence every monent, become a healer of the soul, a lover of *all people*. There is not *one* entity not worth loving. Have compassion for all of them within your soul and love everyone equally. If a man is deaf, his infirmity is no greater than that of the woman who suffers within her soul from feelings of inadequacy and insecurity.

Never recognize in anyone anything other than God and life. Never see imperfection. Never recognize problems. Never see a leper or a cripple as being diseased. When you see only God in others, soon that is all *they* will recognize.

Now, master, hear this: Do *not* desire to go out and heal

others with a touch. Do not desire to be compassionate to anyone before you have been that with yourself. Be who you are
and love yourself *first*, above all things. Love your body.
Honor and respect it. Give to yourself everything you would
give to a great love of your life. Be so loving and compassionate with your *own* being, so pure and unlimited in your
own thought processes, that you are healed in your *own* attitude and your own body. Then you become an example that
motivates others to do the same, if that is their desire.

Become the lord-god of your being. When you do, you will
know that everyone is at the hands of their own creation; that
love lifts them to see further. And when others say to you, "I
see you have a peace about you and a light that surrounds your
total being. Whence come they?" you can smile at them and
say, " 'Tis the Father within me that you see, from the Father
that is within you." Then you are a healer of the attitude, for
you give them the thought that says, "I am perfect, I am
God."

Turn your eyes within, and feel the love of God that is
there. Once you have done that with yourself, you will have
the strength to display your love openly to everyone else, for
you will know who you are and the depths of your love. Then
you heal just by being.

Become the ideal of self *for* self, in spite of everyone else
but *for* everyone else.

One day, master, when you have accepted change and mastered your limitations, you will find love, deep love that you
have never known before, that reaches to the very core of your
being. From that, you will excel into ecstacy, and then into
light. Then you will be God eternal. That is the process, and I
will see that you experience all of it.

Do not become the healer. Become God. Then you are all
things to all people. So be it.

***

15

Release
Your Tormentor

Ramtha: (To a 15-year-old girl who was raped by her step-father) Beautiful lass, who is rushing into womanhood, what say you?

Master: (After a few moments) I don't know what to say.

Ramtha: You don't have to say anything. What do you *feel*? Ponder that for a moment.

Master: I . . . I don't understand what you mean.

Ramtha: What is important is not what you have to say, but how you feel. Feelings I understand. Words were created, lass, only to express the emotions within one's soul.

(After pause) You are in a bit of a conflict, and you are needing direction. I will give it to you. There is a door that needs to be opened to you. I will see that it is opened. But remember, all that is ever important is how you feel.

Now, lass, understand this: All is known. It has been seen, it has been witnessed. The judgment is on the tormentor, for he despises himself for the act. You are now tormenting yourself by your hurt and anger. Release your tormentor, who is you, and begin to be a little girl again.

In your society, little girls have been encouraged to look like women who would tempt the heart of *any* man. But little girls should *stay* little girls for a long time. The same goes for little boys. But here, everything is rushed. Here, children grow up in great conflict, for they don't know what they are supposed to be or how they are supposed to look. If they look anything other than the accepted mode, they are afraid they will be rejected. If they do not act as their peers or parents want them to act, they feel they will not be loved. What a travesty! And here, there are fathers who abuse their daughters, molest them, and do many things to them to prove they are still young and virile men, because in your society and its limited thinking, "youth" is *all* that matters. I find that abominable! *(Tears begin to well in the girl's eyes.)*

Master, understand this: The one who has hurt you is also a child of this society and its direful consciousness. As little boys grow up, they are told to be certain ways, to act certain ways; it is programmed into their beings, so it becomes a part of their consciousness in attitude. And they are always esteemed if they are young and agile and rich. But when their age begins to show and their potency is questioned, often they will turn to young women in order to madly hold on to something they feel they are losing, because they want to be loved and accepted. The same is true with women.

My beautiful master, you are a little girl. A little girl! Yet you don't even know what it's *like* to be a little girl, because from the time you were a young child your life has been the product of rushing to become a grown-up.

Be a little girl and do what the child inside you wishes to do. Make all your dreams come true. Allow yourself to grow gracefully into womanhood rather than running into it. And always keep the child-like simplicity that allows you to love everyone.

If others are adorning themselves to look the image of a woman, do not imitate them. Simply be what you are. Then you will keep your youth a long time, and you will find happiness, *extraordinary* happiness, but not until you release this.

Lass, I hacked men to bits for doing what your father did. I cut their heads off and flung them into the sea. But that never helped anyone. *(The girl begins to weep.)*

I *love* this entity who has hurt you. I love him greatly, for he is a god, and I know *why* he is weak. I am sending a restraint to this entity, and I am dealing with him. But if you hate yourself and this entity, know that you are far more in error than he ever was. •

Nothing has been taken away from you unless you feel that it has. Understand that. Love yourself and forgive the one who has hurt you. This does not mean you must stay with him. But forgive him and forgive yourself, and earnestly love and adore who you are. You are worth all the love you can give to yourself.

What has happened in your past is over. It is no longer of importance. Do not allow scars to rest within your being. There is no need for them to be there. Do not allow your life to be marred by another's hatred of himself, ever. Ever! For then you are victimizing your own being. No one is *worth* the feelings of bitterness or anger.

What do you have to say? Nothing. Your words can do very little to represent your emotions. I understand your emotions. They are not marred; they are still beautiful. For your sake—and *no one else's*—keep them that way; keep the fire burning brightly within your being. Look upon your being and see it as precious, and never lose that image. And never lower yourself by despising anyone. Anyone! Then the love within you will add to your beauty, and you will be a gem beyond measure and, one day, the prize of a sweet and gentle prince.

I will send you runners who will be joyous and happy. Be happy with them. And one day, when the mother of your being can shake loose from her material securities, I will send you both away to a place where you will find extraordinary peace, which is worth much more than any material value that has been gained through this relationship.

Now, we will do a wondrous thing this day. We will restore the body in its completeness. It is a beautiful being. We will remove the scars and restore it. Lass, *you* restore *yourself*. Understand? *(The girl nods.)* So be it.

(After long silence) There once was an age for adolescence,

and it went through one's thirty-third year. Try earnestly to be a child until you are at least 33. Then you will have lived, enjoyed, gained wisdom; you will have learned of evenness, compassion, humility, and who you are. You will never age if you do this, and you will always keep your youthful appearance.

You are greatly loved, lass. Go and run in your fields and have laughter. So be it.

***

16

Yeshua

There has been a prophecy upon your plane for a long time that speaks of the "second coming of Christ." Well, the prophecy is indeed a great truth, and it *will* be fulfilled. But it will not be fulfilled through the return of Yeshua ben Joseph, whom many call Jesus the Christ. Rather, the fulfillment of the prophecy is when the simple teachings exemplified by this great and immaculate soul become a living reality in everyone upon this plane. It is when all people, one by one, realize the truths that Yeshua so arduously endeavored to teach mankind, and then love themselves enough to *live* those truths, steadfastly and boldly, yet humbly.

The christ that is returning is the realization by each of you that you are a divine and immortal principle—that you are, outrageously so, what is termed God. It is christ the fearless, the humble, the lover, the gentle, the noble, coming forward from within you and becoming dominant in your life.

There has never been only *one* christ. "Christ" is an ancient word that simply means "god-man *realized*." Everyone who lives in the flesh is god-man. Everyone upon this plane is a son or daughter of the Father, for everyone is a part of the Mind of God expressing their divine intelligence through the form called humanity. When you *realize* this, you become "the anointed one." Who anoints you? God, to be sure: *your* god—Self! You anoint yourself, *through knowingness*, and dedicate your life to serving the emotions of love and joy.

Now, I wish to enlighten you a little bit about Yeshua ben

Joseph. Though many believe him to be a myth, Yeshua really lived, and he really died, and he really lives again. Eternity now belongs to him. He *earned* the right to be there.

Yeshua became a great christ, indeed. But he was not different from you. He came to this plane just as you came. He was, and is, a son of God and a son of man, just as you are. And he was not *sent* here. He came here of his own choosing, just as many of you have been doing for the ten million years that man has been upon this plane. And Yeshua had the same freedom of will and the same power that you do to embrace the human drama and fulfill yourself in love.

Many things have been written about this entity, writings that have brought forth not only great good but great atrocities upon this plane, which, I can tell you, Yeshua never desired to happen. But let us talk about him as an entity and his purpose for coming to this plane.

Before Yeshua's advent, man had been limited and ruled through fear for eons. Now, fear did not exist in the consciousness of the gods when they first began the adventure of the human drama. Fear became a solidified emotion within the soul when the gods living as man became surviving creatures, subject to the elements, subject to predators, subject indeed to death. When the gods so identified themselves with their bodies and the plane of matter, they soon forgot they were immortal and divine creatures, and they became fearful of *everything*. When they no longer knew that all love, power, and knowingness flowed through them, they began to seek for these outside themselves. Soon, they looked to the stars, priests, and prophets for understanding and knowingness; they looked to leaders, kings, and governments for protection and survival.

Fear has been mankind's greatest enslaver because it has kept you from knowing and expressing who and what you are. It has kept you from experiencing the joy and adventure of life. It has kept you limited by poverty, ignorance, disease, and death. It has kept you on the wheel of life after life upon the plane of density in matter. And when fear exists within your consciousness, the love of God, the love of self, the love of brother to brother, god to god, can never be—can *never* be—for fear chokes off the expression and experience of love. You can never truly love or receive the love of that which you fear. That is a *great* truth.

Yeshua came to this plane for a grand purpose. He came to fulfill a plan devised by an unseen brotherhood who loves you, who watches over and protects this plane of gods living the dream called mankind. The plan was a grand design to help free the people of this plane from the bondage of fear, dogma, laws, and limited beliefs.

Yeshua came to do away with the fear of death, man's greatest fear and the basis of all others. He came to remind you of the God that exists not outside of you but within you—the everlasting principle that forever *loves* you, that forever *is* you, that forever guarantees you eternal life. He came to teach you that your true kingdom is not this plane of matter, but the kingdom of thought and emotion that created and gives meaning to this plane.

Before Yeshua made his advent upon this plane, he chose his mother, who was a member of the Essenes, a sect of the Jewish people, for they were heavily governed by the laws of an entity called Jehovah and the teaching that God is an angry, judgmental, and fearsome entity who exists outside of man.*
an entity called Jehovah and the that God is an angry, judgmental, and fearsome entity who exists outside of man.*

Now, whenever you are born into this plane, it is most arduous to maintain the knowingness of who you truly are, for you are very vulnerable to accepting the beliefs, superstitions, and limited thinking of those you depend upon for nurturance and survival. The same was true with Yeshua. But through great guidance and assistance, and his great determination to

---

*Ramtha has taught that Jehovah is actually an individual, a god, who used his powers to encourage worship of him amongst a group of people of Babylonian descent, who later became the Jewish people.

be an example to this plane, Yeshua never lost the knowingness that he was a son of God, though at times he struggled to
hold on to it.

As a little boy, Yeshua communed with the stars and spoke
to entities not seen by anyone else. And he taught his mother
and father, who were awed at his great wisdom.

From the time he was 12 until he was 30, Yeshua traveled
to many countries and studied under many great entities, who
taught him and reminded him of the very same things I am
teaching you. And he learned about every major religion and
belief system of the time. What did Yeshua come to realize?
That they all altered and limited the understanding of God and
Life; that the truth was *within him*; that God could never be
known through the teachings of men, only through the kingdom of thought and emotion within each entity.

Yeshua was so simple that he was brilliant. He had the
ability to draw great wisdom from his own creative self, because he never looked outside himself for truth. Continuously,
he asked the Father within him for knowingness. That was his
only prayer: "Beloved Father, open me up to know." Because Yeshua had a burning desire to know, he knew *everything*—because he *asked* to know everything! He could look
at you and know everything about you, as *I* look at you and
know everything. That knowingness freed him from this
world, allowed him to wear rags yet feel like a king, and filled
him with love that encompassed *all people*, even beggars and
warmongers, even prostitutes and centurions. It gave him the
power to turn water into wine, to heal the sick, raise the
dead—to manifest *whatever* he desired, just by a turn of his
thought and the embrace of emotion.

Yeshua's intense desire to live as a son of man and still express his godhood drove him to master the human drama. Realizing the truth of self and living it steadfastly was his chosen
path. It is the same path many of you have chosen in this
lifetime. And the fire of becoming yourself, the burning away
of the illusions of self that all of you are experiencing, is the

same fire Yeshua experienced.

Yeshua mastered and mastered his limitations of thought to become himself, the god within, his own messiah. Through a simple and uncomplicated mind, he learned to look at life through the eyes of a child, to see only God in all people and all things, to find peace and joy in each moment, regardless of the world outside and all of its frantic illusions—the simple things I am teaching you this day. Because they were simply *the* truth for Yeshua, they became *law*, *his* law for the rule of his *own* kingdom. And his law allowed him to step out of the prison of fear, out of the box of limited beliefs, bigotry, and judgment, into the heaven of emotion and life forever.

Why did Yeshua go into the wilderness? To confront Satan. But *who* is Satan? It is not an entity that lives *outside* of you! It is your altered ego, the altered thinking created by your immersion in the plane of matter. Satan is your altered identity, which tempts you into thinking that this illusion is the steadfast reality. It is thinking that beauty, power, joy, and fulfillment lie outside of you. It is fear, doubt, self-judgment and self-denial. Satan is all things that keep you from receiving the love and joy that continuously flow from God the Father.

Yeshua went to the wilderness to confront *himself*. He went there to purge from himself every limited thought, so he would be so aligned within himself that his greatest desire was all he saw before him. He fasted for 40 days and 40 nights, and he mastered his body. He overcame the temptation to rule his brothers and to possess the limited ideals of this plane. For with the power within him that he had learned to use, he could have had the fame and riches that man lusted for; he even could have had dominion over every nation of the world. *Great* temptations. But Yeshua never lost sight of his purpose for coming here, which was to exemplify what it is to *live* as God; to demonstrate the power of god within man to have victory over death; and to free the people from the laws of man, so that their love for God within mankind would be the sole governing force in their lives.

In 40 days of expression, with *intense* emotion and *great* fire, Yeshua purged his temptations by living through them in thought. He embraced the feeling of all of them, gained the wisdom from that embrace, and allowed them to be fulfilled.

Yeshua came out of the wilderness with great strength and clarity of purpose. He began traveling about the countryside performing miracles and teaching all that "The kingdom of heaven is here, for the kingdom of heaven is within you." And it *is*, my beloved masters, because *within you* is joy born; *within you* do answers come; *within you* do miracles occur. The kingdom of heaven is not some far-off place you go to when you leave this plane! You are already *in* it! For heaven is your capacity to have peace, joy, and love in your life, each and every moment, simply by what you think.

Yeshua gathered his disciples and began to teach them what he had taught himself, for they were to carry on the teachings after his crucifixion, which was also part of the plan. He told them, "I have come here to fulfill the prophecy." Well, they were all in agreement that *he* was the one fulfilling the prophecy. Then he said to them, "If God can come upon earth and walk as man, then he understands the weaknesses and the strengths of man." They all agreed that was true, since they had seen great love, compassion, and understanding demonstrated by Yeshua.

He told them, blatantly, "I am the son of God." But *never* did he say that he was the *only* son of God. He never said he was the messiah. He never even said he was a christ. He *did* say that he and the Father were one and the same, a most blasphemous statement! And he never moved from that center, ever! And he told them, "*You* are the sons of God also. Know that the Father dwells within you, for the Father and you are also one."

To this, the disciples shook their heads and said, "But how it is that God can be *us*?" "*Know* that God is there," Yeshua answered. "*Know* that is a truth; then you will realize that truth."

Then Yeshua made it even more pronounced: "*All* people are God. Even your *enemies* are God. Even nations unknown to you, children unborn, are God." Not once, *ever*, did Yeshua utter that the whole of mankind were not also gods, not also sons.

All the miracles and wonders he performed, he did to teach of the power of God within all people. He told his disciples, "What I have done, *you* can do, for the Father within us is the power to do and be all things." Yeshua told them that if they were steadfast in who they were and what they desired—if they did not succumb to doubt but *trusted* the Father within them implicitly—whatsoever they dreamed in the kingdom within them would be theirs.

Yeshua told the people and his disciples, "With my coming I have done away with the scriptures, for I have come to fulfill the law." He taught them of the hypocrisy of the laws of Moses, for they governed only the outward actions of men, not their thoughts and feelings. He told them, "To enter the kingdom of heaven, the only laws you need to obey are to love the Father within you with all of your heart, and to love your neighbor as you love yourself. To obey the laws of your Father is to obey them not only in the physical but also within the soul. If you even think a thought against another, unto the soul of your being, it is the same as having done it. And by virtue of that thought, you have separated yourself from your Father's kingdom, which is the feelings within you."

Yeshua taught the people and his disciples in every way that he could for them to understand, simply, that the Father and the kingdom of heaven were indeed within them. But they *still* had difficulty understanding, because they had been taught for so many lifetimes that they were merely servants to a god that lived outside of the human creature. They had been taught that the kingdom of heaven shall descend onto the earth plane, God will walk amongst the good, and the oppressors of Judea and Israel will be banished forever. Of course! That was the dream of the Jewish people.

Yeshua spent arduous moments teaching his disciples and demonstrating his teachings over and over again. But they would not allow the truth of what he was saying to fully manifest within them, because it would mean that they, too, would have to be the simple, pure, immaculate entity that Yeshua was.

All throughout his ministry, Yeshua took counsel with great entities in the unseen. Often he would go into the wilderness, where he would learn and then return to teach what he had learned. In his last days, Yeshua took counsel more often for renewed strength. For while he was loved by many, he was despised by many more, and he was becoming vulnerable to the hatred, doubt, and negativity that was all around him. How many more miracles must he perform to prove that what he was saying was a truth?

Yeshua's greatest test and his greatest mastery was to demonstrate the victory of the human spirit over death. He chose to die on his tree to show the people that he, god-man, lived in spite of death; that he could take his body and resurrect it. He chose to die, reassemble his body, and return to his disciples in manifested form to say, "You see, you *do* live forever."

For three days following his crucifixion, Yeshua appeared to his disciples, and he taught them and encouraged them. On the last day, he gathered them together by the sea of Galilee, and there gave them their last teaching: "Live what I have taught you. Know that the Father and the kingdom of heaven, which are within me, have always been within you. Go and do the works I have done, even greater, and be an example and a light to the world."

Yeshua told them of his love for them, and encouraged them to fear nothing, not Rome or Caesar or Herod or the sword: "Fear *nothing*, for you will live forever." And he told them he would be with them until the end of time, when he would return—which is a great truth.

With that, the master rose 30 feet above the earth, became a brilliant light, and the whole sky lit up. In that moment,

Yeshua ascended, for one who knows he is God has the ability to transform matter and transcend all things. He went into an unseen dimension of life, as everyone does, but he took his body with him so that he could return to this plane anytime he chose without having to go through the birth process.

The reason Yeshua left was that it was time for the disciples to lead rather than follow. Yet they ended up following anyway, and becoming immersed in the limitations of thought from which Yeshua strove to free them. His disciples never became as he was in that life, because they never fully understood what Yeshua was teaching. They did not have the courage to master their limitations and be like the immaculate entity they loved. So they began to teach the people that Yeshua was the *only* miracle worker, the only christ, the only son of God. They hailed him as "Savior, Lord of Hosts, King of Kings"—whatever tribute they could give to Yeshua to elevate him above them. And so, many began to *worship* Yeshua ben Joseph in the name of Jesus the Christ. By doing so, they put all of the burden for the salvation of the world upon the shoulders of Yeshua, giving away their power and ability to be their own salvation through the christ within themselves.

Soon, the miracles were lost to mankind, the teachings were changed, and mankind remained enslaved by religious dogma and governmental rule. And for centuries to come, bloody religious wars would encompass your world, and innocents would be maimed and slaughtered in the name of Yeshua ben Joseph, the great christ who came to this plane to foster love between all people.

But Yeshua did fulfill the prophecy, for he did away with the laws of Jehovah and created the Law of One, the law of "oneness within," which means, "The Father and you are one." He lived as man, died a very cruel death, and resurrected his body to prove a point—and he proved it well. He did not die for the sins of the world, but for the freedom of the world from the great deceiver, which is fear. He did not teach of hell or Lucifer or a fearsome God. He did not teach of the

inequality or separateness of people. He never set up the
Church, nor did he teach of dogma, rules, or rituals. He taught
only of the Father that lives within man, and he openly demonstrated that intelligence, that power and beauty and un-
bounded love.

Yeshua became a hero to this plane because he lived and
aligned himself with an unlimited truth and demonstrated it
openly. He devoted his life to becoming *wholly* who he was,
and so he did. His nobleness was that he *lived* his knowingness and was not afraid to speak it. He overcame the intimida-
tion of his parents' people and the temple priests, because his
love for himself and the people of this plane was all that was
important to him. So great was his love for God and his own
association with being a son of God, that he resurrected himself through the power of thought. He took his knowingness
all the way through death, profoundly and impeccably never
moving from his knowingness, and he went into eternity, into
a joy and adventure that is beyond description.

Although history and the weaknesses of men have greatly
altered what Yeshua taught, his teaching is still simple. It is to
allow yourself to *be who you are*! For when you are the isness
of yourself, the I AM principle, you realize the joy and peace
of the Father within you. And when you know that you are
eternal, that the Father within you *is* forever, nothing can ever
inhibit you from becoming who you are. For how can one ever
enslave, intimidate, or rule an entity who fears nothing, not
even death? That, indeed, is salvation. That is when love
flows outward from every fiber of your being.

Yeshua experienced and mastered every agony man could
have, every weakness that man possesses, and came forth tri-
umphant. But what he did, you can do also, for the Father that
lives within him lives within you equally. And the love and
power that he possesses is the same that you possess.

For ages, you have worshiped entities because of their
straightforwardness, their nobility of spirit, their courage to
overcome great difficulty. But who are *you*? Do you not have

the courage to become who *you* are and to live your truth blatantly?

Many of you worship Yeshua and the agony he suffered. You continuously put him on the cross, let him hang upon your walls and around your neck. Why? Why do you continuously want to see him suffer? Because it justifies your own suffering? Yeshua already had his time, he already hung from a miserable tree. Do not keep him on it. He doesn't *belong* there. Do not worship his agony; that is a symbol of enslavement. Do not worship his *death*—embrace his *life*!

This simple entity was a man, just like you. What he became, *you* will eventually become, for what he desired to accomplish, you will eventually desire. But you cannot realize what Yeshua realized if you place the responsibility on his shoulders for *your* hypocrisy and illusions. They don't belong to *him*; they belong to you!

Yeshua is not responsible for saving you or this plane. He was the savior of *himself*, through *knowingness*. And what he knew, he did not learn from teachers or scriptures, from ritualistic practices or dogmatic understandings, but from the personalized god-force within him. He gained all he knew by listening wholly to the voice within him and going with that knowingness in spite of ridicule, criticism, even death.

In this time, I am your teacher and your runner who has come to tell you this: The christ that you have loved, that many have worshiped, that many have kept on his cross because it reminds them of their guilt, loves each of you equally, as one brother to another. He still lives, and is even here on this plane. He lives and will forever live, because he has become the principle I AM. One day, when all on this plane take his teachings to heart and begin to love their own god within them, then the beloved Yeshua will return. For then he will not be worshiped or idolized any longer. You will have taken him off the cross and allowed him to be a living brother to you, for you will know that you are no less than he.

Do not *worship* Yeshua, *love* him! Love the ideal you see in him, and become that ideal yourself. When others ask, "Where is your kingdom?" tell them, blatantly, "My kingdom is not of this world. It is within me." And when they ask, "Who is your God?" have the courage to say, "I am the lord-god of my being, for the Father and I are one." Then you are one with this great master. Then you are enlightened, and that knowledge has allowed you to be an entity who can look fear in the face and spit in its eye, for in the times that are coming you are going to need to do just that.

Yeshua embraced life through a nobility of spirit and the wisdom he gained from within him. That wisdom allowed him to conquer and master all things, even death. It allowed him to hang upon a cross and, despite the tearing of flesh and the agonies of his body, look over his shoulder at the people and love them. That strength does not come from your parents, your neighbors, or anyone else. It comes wholly from the Father within you—the intelligence, the emotion that allows you to overcome all things.

When you love yourself enough to rise above dogma, social consciousness, and the cloistered thinking of man, and go within to realize your own divinity and immortality, then you will have the strength to be grander than fear, grander than judgment, grander than self-denial. When you love what you are—and in such utter peace that the benevolence of God within you is real, more *real* than your illusions—then you will have the strength to love and embrace all humanity, however they are expressing, and allow them to be, as your Father has allowed you to be.

Your plane has been searching for peace and love, but it can only have these when each of you becomes them within your *own* kingdom, within your own voyage of thought. When you become that, wholly for your own joy, you become an example for others. To offer even one entity another avenue of thought is a grand thing, for in doing that, you have helped to expand consciousness into a greater understanding. When you listen only to the voice within you and live the truth that self has to offer, you help your beloved brothers to have the courage to look within themselves and find the goodness and the beauty that they truly are. Then, one by one, mankind returns to its sovereignty. That is imminent on your plane—and these are *not* just pretty words.

Become *your* ideal, whatever that is for your own purposeful being, and *live* the god that you are. *Live* your knowingness! That living emits strength. And when there is strength, there is the courage to receive and give forth life.

Know that you are forever. Unless you know that you are greater than death, you will be enslaved by fear all of your life. As long as you are dominated by fear, you can never know the kingdom of heaven, for the love of God and the joy of life are utterly without fear. That is why *no thing* is worth fearing.

Those of you who do not desire to embrace life with the innocence of a child, I leave you to the kingdom of Man and its stagnated consciousness. Those of you who desire to learn, I will show you a magnificent kingdom and a new life.

Your times are changing, and they are challenging, indeed. To embark upon the changes that are coming, you must know the grandness of what is coming. That cannot be ascertained if you allow fear or judgment to intimidate you out of your knowingness. If you cannot find the vibrance and joy of life in each moment, in the days that are coming you will fall to the fear that will run rampant in social consciousness.

Do away with fear. Overcome and overcome your limitations of thought until you become a fearless entity and a manifesting god who sits within his kingdom in joy and peace. Then you will live to see the meek inherit this earth, for those times are nigh upon the land.

Love Yeshua ben Joseph, the great christ, but love yourself more so that you can become what he became. When you love yourself, you embrace God within. When you love yourself,

Christ walks again.

I salute you from the lord-god of my being. Go and live your light. I will always be with you. So be it!

***

17

A Place Such As This

This is my wondrous temple. Here, where there is quiet, I see the stars that speak no word. I see the solemnness of mountains that are steadfast and speak no word. I see the bush that bends and shivers in the wind, yet speaks no word. Only the wind plays amongst that which is steadfast and quiet, that allows you to be however you are so you can become as they—quiet, constant, allowing, forgiving. It was through such quiet and beauty that I, Ramtha, found the Unknown God and reasoned into myself dignity and honor.

No man can give you the openness, the divine respect, or the permissiveness that allows you to become what you are. Nothing can do that as the wilderness can. I bless this temple, for it allows man to remember who he truly is.

The night sky, how wondrous it is! For it permits you to see the spectacle of stars, sparkling like brilliant jewels against the backdrop of forever. It is indeed beautiful!

When I was a little boy, I did not know that the stars were other places. I thought they were the children of the moon, the Enchantress, and that one day they would grow up, and we would have *many* great moons. Well, I am not disappointed that it isn't so. I am pleased for the virtue of my innocence and

---

This chapter presents an address spoken on a hilltop overlooking the Yucca Valley desert in California as the sun set behind the mountains.

135

my ability to imagine such a wonderful fantasy.

Look at the sky. Many of you never see it. You only know it is there and expect it to still be there if ever you look upon it. But you never do, nor do you ever give gratitude to it. Yet the evening sky, resting upon purpled mountains and the quiet valley below—it is God! Look upon it and contemplate for a moment how many splendid sunsets there have been since the beginning of time . . . and how many of them you have missed.

Entities often gravitate to this memory only when they are soon to pass from this plane. And when they look at the evening sky, they weep dearly from their souls. For shall they ever see another evening? Shall they ever see another tomorrow? They have lived fast and furious, and they failed to look upon the blessed beauty that was all around them. But in the moments before their passing, they now want to hold on to each spectacular moment, because as the gold fades from the sky, long shall this view be lost to them, and what awaits them in the morning, they know not.

If one can take the moments throughout his life to appreciate the blatant, continuous beauty around him, without having to capture it before he dies, then long will he live and great will be the wisdom that will come to him for recognizing such simple splendor. Take a great lesson from those who meet their last hour holding on to life, because the things that were allowed to be so unimportant are now held very dear.

Three things did those of my soldiers who were perishing from mortal wounds always weep for as their final hour was upon them. One was their beloved mother, because from the thrust of her womb they came into this world, and in her simple nurturing and caring for them—regardless of the defiance they displayed—she loved them throughout their lives. Thus, in the moment when utter helplessness came upon them, many called out for their mothers, whom they outgrew during their robust manhood, but now, upon the ending of their lives, needed to hold on to and embrace.

Others wept for their lovers or their wives, the reflections of themselves in subdued beauty, whom they were soon to be without. They called out to their women to please love them, hold them, give them all they could in the short time left. And their women, in great strength and compassion, came to their sides and embraced them, nurtured them, loved them. And they wept in the arms of their women.

Others cried out to me, "Ramtha, wondrous Ram, where go I? Speak to this God that you have pursued in your damnable madness, that which I have cursed because it has taken you from me, and ask that he receive me." I spoke to them, embraced them, and allowed them to feel love, for where they were going *is* love.

In watching my my people's passings, it always seemed a pity to see them reach out in their final moments for the things they never made time for in their lives. And I reasoned with that as I observed the pure, continuous beauty around me. I watched it from early morn until early morn. I was caught up in it for what you term years. Years! And it was through observing children and lovers and evening skies—the things so many reached out for before they died—that I gained great wisdom and understanding about life, its reasons, its purpose, its nature.

A wise and wondrous teacher am I, but I did not become that through the teachings of man. I became that by being a part of the *whole* of all that God is—not by fighting or warring against it, but by flowing with it.

Regardless of the values you call important, what you urgently need in your being is to appreciate what you are in relationship to this plane, for this plane is the only one where you can relate to the whole of what God is.

Many of you are enslaved by your work. You are like my soldiers who were enslaved to war and battle, for they felt that fighting was their only purpose in life. If you do not become *un*involved with the labors that hard-press and enslave you, you shan't ever realize the glory of your existence. If it is not within you to be solitary in such a wilderness, you will always be like the animals, faceless and lost among the herd.

If you do not have the patience to go to a wilderness such as this and leave your sword and your troubles behind you, I tell you, evenly, you will run swiftly to your death. And the hour before you gasp your last breath, you will desire that it could last forever, so that you could experience what you never took time to experience, and have the moments to contemplate yourself and your life.

• Learn to detach yourself from the things that demand of you, that enslave you, that blind you to the power and beauty within. Learn to change. Leave behind your enslavements and go to a consciousness such as this. Here it is holy, indeed, and the Father can be seen more readily in the day-to-day ongoingness of life. Here in the quiet, in the wind, in the dew, the voice of God will speak to you; it will wake you out of your slumber, the hypnotic influence of your creations, and allow you to see more clearly. Had I not done this, no one would have ever heard of me, and none of you would have, locked wonderfully in your souls, the memory of Ramtha and the knowingness of what I taught you long ago.

In a wilderness such as this, I sat on a rock for seven years before making my next move. But when I made it, it was the right one. I *knew* where to go and who to go to. What I heard was not a voice, such as I speak to you. It was the pure consciousness *allowed* in a place such as this. That feeling spoke to me, and I fed from it. And the more I felt, the more I wanted. That is how I obtained wisdom.

• In your holidays, instead of rushing to encumber yourselves in activities, go to a place such as this, and sit and observe and be. This will enlighten you greatly, even if done for but a few days. The realizations that will occur will take you from your rut, your enslavements, and give you the strength to re-create your life. And whenever you come under the spell of the sorcerers called time and labor, go to a place such as this and listen for a few more days. When you return, you will be refreshed and invigorated.

Take time to experience this consciousness. Do not think that this existence must be a yoke around your neck and that you must stay hard-pressed at the plow. Life was never intended to be that way. Realize that you *chose* to be enslaved to your creations through the process of contemplating them. By the same token, realize that you have the option to contemplate your way back out of your enslavements.

Learn to flow with this consciousness. Look at yourself and be even with who you are. Invite change into your life. It will get rid of your stagnation and bring to your life a grand purpose, new creative values, hope, and joy. Do not wait until the moment before you perish to reflect upon such wondrous ideals. Make them a part of your existence now.

***

18

Never Believe

Ramtha: (To an elderly woman) Most patient lady, what say you?

Master: Ramtha, I am *flabbergasted* by your wisdom and your love of God and man!

Ramtha: Flabbergasted?

Master: Yes! I'm so amazed! It's beyond any description.

I think an honest confession is good for the soul, and I don't mind telling you I have been *skeptical* of the love and all the powers I was told you have.

Ramtha: Are you still?

Master: No.

Ramtha: Well, most are skeptical at first because they have been taught to use their intellect to determine truth and reality rather than their feelings, which is the greater intelligence within them.

You are flabbergasted, eh? Well, I will tell you, wondrous woman, not one word has been uttered here that *you* do not know and cannot speak once you remove the limitations of thought that keep you from doing so. *(Shaking his head)* "Flabbergasted, indeed!"

Master: (Chuckling) I knew that would get you!

Ramtha: I am indeed gotten!

Master, the love I feel for you and all entities is a *great* reality—greater, perhaps, than my wisdom, for my love *gave* me my wisdom.

God is *everything*. He is the bloom and its color. He is the laughter and tears of lovers. He is warriors in battle. He is the storm brewing on the horizon. All you have to do is embrace that understanding, and soon the reality of it will come into full view. Then you will have the same profound wisdom also. It is *already* there. It has just been clouded over by your acceptance of limited beliefs.

And my powers? Well, everyone possesses powers. What keeps them from realizing their powers is that they depend upon their flapping mouths and their hands to make miracles. So they feel very limited. But the truth is, *thought* makes the miracles, and the mouth calls them into being. One day, when you truly realize the power of your own thought processes, you too will become a miracle worker and a manifesting god. In the meantime, I desire for you to ponder all of this flabbergasting wisdom, and if you like it, make it your own. It is yours to do with as you will.

Now, most who come into my audience are skeptical, certainly. If they leave still skeptical, it is quite all right. The important thing is that I have spoken to their souls, and everything that has been spoken, they now possess.

If entities do not desire to return to my audiences, that does not mean they are not loved; they will *always* be loved. If they never come back, but they call my name, even a hundred years from now, I will answer them. Those who do come back, come back to learn more and more. As long as they desire to learn, I will teach them, for I love them greatly. Even if only a handful come back, they will become God, because they *desire* to, and they will have a profound impact upon this plane.

Yeshua had only 12 disciples who influenced an entire world. Buddha had a *smaller* gathering, and yet in parts of the world his teachings have reached into hundreds of generations.

Those who stay will be taught, and they will learn. And I

will take them from limited man to great gods who resemble little children but who possess profound knowingness. Then they will do a bit of flabbergasting on their own.

Master, I am pleased you have come here this day. I assure you, you will learn of the extraordinary when you come here, for no one else teaches it. They are frightened to do so, or even to think about it! But as long as you come, even if it is only you who comes, whatever you desire to know I will teach you. And you will experience the emotional aspects of that knowledge. Then, that which I have taught you will not be a belief or a philosophy, but a felt reality, a knowingness.

For ages the people of this plane have been intimidated into *believing* in things that have no basis in reality. Well, I shan't ever desire for you or anyone else to *believe* in what I teach you—indeed, in *anything*. I want you to *know* that what I speak is true. For to know it, you have to experience the manifestation of the knowledge; then it is completely understood and solidified in your soul as an emotion. Do you understand?

Master: Yes, I think so. But I am afraid I have a great deal to learn.

Ramtha: Lady, *everyone* has much to learn. But what is of particular urgency is for you to understand your rights as a human being, as a *god* being, and to know that you have options in this life.

I have come here, not to change your mind, but to engage you into *knowledge*, so the wonderments of that knowledge can come to pass. I am here to help you *realize* that God is omnipresent right within you, right wherever you are; that *you* are the grandest temple of God; that *your life* is the *only* thing that is important—not living by the rules, beliefs, or opinions of other entities, but living in freedom to uniquely express your divine self. And no man, no law, no country can ever give you that freedom. *You already own it!* But continually, you give it away! Every day, you give up your freedom to honor your fears. But what is there to fear? Nothing! You are a forever entity. I'm here to help you realize that, and to teach you how to take back your kingdom, if that is your desire.

You will be ridiculed for listening to such as I, and I shan't have you or anyone else belittled for my sake or hurt because you *believed* in me. I want you to *know* that what is spoken *is* a reality—for you and your life—and then live these understandings to the greatest example you can.

Difficult times are coming upon this plane, and they are nigh at your door. The world is going to need entities who are strong in their knowingness of who and what they are. It is going to need entities who have a certainty of their truth rather than fragile beliefs that can be easily toppled by a strong wind.

I only want you to be *happy*, and to know the Father *loves* you, regardless of what you think, feel, or do. That is all that *needs* to be learned here. If you gain nothing else from this audience, never stop loving yourself, caring about yourself, and wanting to understand better who you are and who the Father is in relationship to you.

But I desire that you never *believe* in what I teach you, ever. I want you to *know*, so what you hear can become a reality. And if it hasn't become a reality yet, then there is an adventure waiting to be lived. You understand?

Master: Yes.

Ramtha: I will send you a runner, lady, who will teach you of the joy of freedom. So be it.

***

19

You Will Never Imprison Their Minds

Let us talk about the laws of your land and the breaking of laws that are limited.

God, the unlimited thought process, the open-ended Isness, is indeed *lawless*. Unlike your governments that possess articles of law, the Father does not—cannot—restrict the thoughts and the manifestation of the thoughts that constitute his Being. God is so lawless he has *allowed* law to be. Man alone is the lawgiver. Only man, living in a limited sphere, creates the regulation of laws to govern the actions of entities.

To be the unlimited essence that God is, which I am teaching all to be, means to be lawless. To be lawless is to be unlimited *in thought*, in your thinking processes. It means to be without any thought, ideal, or attitude that restricts or limits the thoughts you entertain, thus restricting the feeling of thoughts. To become unlimited in your thinking is imperative in order to become the sublime emotion that God is.

Those of you who, in the process of becoming unlimited, deem it acceptable to break the laws of your land, know that you will be even *more* limited than you were before you took such action. Because by that action, you have given credence, you have given power to the thought that your freedom, your joy, your unlimitedness, your godhood, lies *outside* of your being and not *within* you. What in the world is worth being more limited for? Nothing! *No thing.*

Masters, understand this: Freedom comes from within. Freedom must be acknowledged from *within* you, by knowing that you are always free to *have* principles, that you are always free to be honorable and noble in your character, that you are always free to respect and love yourself and others, that you are always free to think any thought and live in the *emotion* of that thought. That is freedom. That is being unlimited. That is joy. That is what allows you always to be in the kingdom of heaven that is, indeed, *within you*.

There are great masters, sublime gods, who live under the most oppressive, the most restrictive governments of your world, yet they are still free. They are *still* free! Though you may put them into prison, you will never imprison their minds and their thinking. Through the unlimitedness of their thought processes, they will experience the joy and the freedom that so many of you, even in this great land of yours, are struggling so arduously to attain. You may even threaten to hack off their heads, but will that intimidate them and take them from the joy of the moment? Nay. For a master *knows* he is forever, that his kingdom is *ongoing Thought*.

In your government that you have put forth "of the people, by the people, for the people," as it is termed, the *people*, which you are, constitute the regulation of law. If you have chosen to live within the perimeters of this country, you have openly accepted its laws, and it would behoove you to abide by them in regard to your relations with other entities.

If you have chosen to live in this kingdom, then *love* it. Love your decision to be here. If there is a law or regulation that you are not pleased with, or that you feel you cannot allow to be, then *change it*, but do so through *peaceful* means. You have the *power* within you to do it!

Be righteous. "Righteous" means the *right use* of self. That means abiding by the freedom within you to be blessed, noble, and honorable in your character, in your deeds, and your actions.

Love your country "of the people, by the people, and for

the people.'' It is a wondrous country. Love the lawmakers. *You* are the lawmakers. Abide by the laws of your country. If you don't like them, change them. If you do not wish to change them, honor them or seek you out another land. But always allow yourself the freedom to be unlimited in your thinking. So be it.

***

20

Reclaiming
Your Power

Know you what "want" is? You should. It's the most often used word in your language. All of you want, want, want! Well, that is all right, because "want" sets the wheels of manifestation into motion.

I desire for you to be a light to this world. You are approaching epic moments when your plane is going to need it. To become that, you must learn the greatest knowledge and then master your limitations of thought. But you can do that only when you are ready for it. You have to *want* to be a master. You have to *want* to master your life. Know how you wanted everything else in your dream? Fame, fortune, beauty, lovers, clothing, hovels? It's the *same* want. If you put the *same* power behind wanting to be a master as you have done for tedious, petty things in your dream, you'll become the all-wise, knowing intelligence.

In my life, I *wanted* it. I didn't know what it was I wanted, I just wanted it. And perhaps the grandest manifestations come from the imageless want.

Now, I look at your lives, and I see your hang-ups and hang-downs, your limitations, your predicaments, your illnesses, and I see who created them. You did. Everything you are in this dream, you are because you wanted to be that

---

Excerpted and edited from *Ramtha Intensive: Soulmates*.

way. Whether you are rich or poor, king or beggar; whether you are married, unmarried, seeking, secure, happy, or unhappy; you created it, you made it that way; you wanted to experience that for the end result called *emotional wisdom*. So, it is not the games of *action* that have been important, but the treasure of *re*-action, called wisdom. And all of you have gained the treasure of your experiences, except it hasn't fully become wisdom yet, because it's still clouded over by guilt, insecurity, blame, and feelings of failure.

Some of you are terribly unhappy; I see it in you. Well, I have no pity for you because I see, in a greater understanding, that you set it up, you wanted it that way. You want to feel the way you are feeling. Only when you *want* your life to be different will you change. Nothing—no one, no power, not even I, with all the runners, miracles, and knowledge—can change your stubborn minds. Because, you see, the key to the door of understanding is on *your* side of the door. You are a god, and whatever you desire for your kingdom, so it is! That one and only law can never be disputed or overridden.

Many of you say you are "messed up" in your minds. Guess *who* messed you up? Take hold of the responsibility! It *belongs* to you. How do you unmess yourself? Want it! There is not *one* problem you have that cannot be changed in a twinkling of an eye. Not one!

Know you joy? Joy is the great treasure of feeling. Yet there are a host of you here who have *never* known this paradise of emotion. You have known the burst of laughter from crude jokes and the like, but you have never been lifted and happy at all moments because you are living in a state of *being*. There is always something that brings you down—and *you* create those things yourselves. If your children or your husband make you unhappy, it's because you have *allowed* them to. You have allowed your happiness to be centered on *them* rather than *you*. If they make you unhappy, you have given your power away to them, because anything outside of you that you allow to determine your *re*-action, you give your power to. Did you know that?

Joy is *self*-realized. Joy is the result of *sovereignty*, and it draws your power back to you. A master wakes up from the dream he has been living and begins to become sovereign again; he begins to reclaim his power to make himself *happy*.

To become sovereign, a master's first realization is that he created his life the way he wanted it. He becomes *aware* that he chose *everything*. That awareness increases his power, and he is waking up from the dream. When you take responsibility for your life and know that you created everything in your kingdom, that you allowed it to occur, it will set you free from guilt, blame, and hatred. It will allow you to own the wisdom of this dream. It will bring peace and joy home to you.

Now, you want to manifest? You want to turn water into wine? You want to manifest bread in your hand or gold in your treasury? Whenever you become part of a following, a group or sect or cult, you give away the power to do that.

You will never become sovereign in a *group*! You become sovereign *individually*. Unlimited, outrageous mind becomes only when one is wholly in tune with *self*. Now you know why a master walks alone.

A master never asks another for answers, because he knows that every moment he does, he removes himself from knowingness. A master *knows* his destiny, because a master possesses the *power* of the awakening christ. All he has to do is ponder and desire, and whatever he desires to know is revealed to him within a moment; whatever he desires his future to be, so it is.

You wanted to find the greatest teacher? I *am* the greatest teacher, *in my reality*. I have no difficulty telling you that. But the greatest teacher to *you* is the god within that makes you "you." If you start to give your power away to me by worshiping me, or putting the responsibility for your learning on *my* back, I shall send you from this audience straightaway. Do you understand? *(Audience members nod.)*

There is no one in the seen or unseen who is greater than

you. You have dreamed them to be such, and you have worshiped them; you have become subservient to them. No wonder you can't manifest anything! You don't have enough power left to pluck a fly off your nose! That is because you have followed the teachings of other entities for *eons*. And when you follow, you learn only about following. So, you're all very good at following, but you don't know how to lead. And leading does not mean gathering little groupies together and marching them off to some place. It means leading *self*: *self*-vision.

It is the time for you to follow *yourself* and the christ that is latent within you. To take back your power, ask only yourself for advice. No one else knows the answer greater than your god knows, because the question *is* the answer. From the lord-god of your being, ask the Father within you for knowingness, and he will manifest it for you—and it is *all* customized! Ask the Father within you for clarity, and then just be, and allow it to come. When you least expect it, you will be *illuminated*. You will know the answer beyond words; it is wisdom now in your soul, another pearl to take home with you.

A master becomes aware, reclaims, and becomes. Becomes! What are you becoming? Free! To become that, you don't have to be anything in particular, you only have to *be*; that is owning *all* of your power, by allowing. You don't have to *do* anything to become. You don't have to meditate or chant until you're hoarse; you only have to *want* to be. The soul of your being will then manifest for you whatever is needed for you to be that.

A master always *is*. A master loves, certainly, and his love for other entities is *unconditional*. But a master always holds on to himself, because the more he does, the greater is his healing power to the world.

You become God and a christ *for yourself*—in spite of the world yet *for* the world. In other words, *you come first*—you and your god. The rest of the world will just have to wait until the process of be-coming is "just wonderful."

Now, another great teaching you should know: There is no such thing as *un*truth. In the All-in-All, there is no such thing as *un*-All. Everything is true, because whatever one thinks, he feels; and whatever is felt, is reality in his kingdom. A person can change his truth any moment, for whenever he changes his mind, he changes his feelings. And if his feelings are changed, he has taken on a new truth, a new reality, and he will react accordingly.

Everyone is right, because everyone is a god who has the freedom to create his own truth, thus his own reality. The person who does not believe in God is right. The person who *hates* you is right. These are staunch teachings, but a master understands.

There are those whose reality is that *they* have the *only* truth; it is called dogma. Did you know that they're right? Their dogma *is* a reality—to them. It becomes *your* reality only if you *accept* it.

If you desire to become the Is, you must allow others their truth. If you do not *want* to, then you become involved in their polarity; you become a warrior. If you judge and persecute them for *their* truth, you will never know your own, for you will be blinded by and enslaved to your judgment of them. Giving your power away is also done by condemning others for what they believe.

What does it mean "to be a light"? It means *living* your truth, *your* reality. Truth is not something you *speak*, it is something you *live*. And the virtues that go along with living your truth are allowing others to be and loving them in freedom. When you love others by allowing them the freedom to hold and express their own truths, you are a light to those who *want* to see your truth.

Understand the nature of people and their convictions. Love them and allow them. If it means standing alone in your own truth and being true to the Father within you—if listening to *your* knowingness means that there shan't be anyone standing beside you—then *stand alone*; it will be *worth* it! *(Picks up his glass and toasts the audience)* To freedom.

Now, I desire to give you a teaching regarding "spiritual truths," because there are many of you here who call yourself "spiritual" entities, don't you? Did you know that's a limitation? If you say you are "spiritual," you have given your power away to another illusion—because *everything* is spiritual; there isn't *one* thing that isn't!

Spiritual entities have their own set of dogmas. But if you believe in karma, you are setting your destiny in stone. If you believe in sin, you are doomed, certainly. If you believe that reincarnation, the wheel-of-life, is the utopia of continuous living, you are of a limited mind—because there is *more* beyond the wheel, such as you cannot imagine! If you believe you are part of a "soul family," you are committing yourself to being with the same old souls, without the exploration of the human drama in all of its beauty.

Some of you have "multudious" guides—and they're *always* aristocrats! And the more guides you have, the more special you feel. Well, that is another dogma, a spiritual dogma.

Do you know *who* your guides are? You! "A-w-w-w." *(Audience laughs)* You do not have to agree with me. You can hang on to those entities if you want to. But if you are a sovereign god, you don't *need* a guide—especially 42 of them!

Your great guide is the spirit of your being. It is the light that surrounds your body. It was the first light of creation, and it is called the blue corona. If you did not have that grand light around you, you would float off into knowingness, cell by cell. What keeps you together? What is the glue? It is called *love*. It is Thought, which is God, in the form of Light.

Your scientists have photographed the lower electrum of this wondrous light field. But your photography is not swift enough to capture the greater light, the higher frequency of the blue corona, which goes very far out. For one who is a master, his light can be nigh three miles in diameter. For one who is closed-minded, his light is very close to his body because his thoughts are heavily focused in material density.

Oftentimes entities see their own spirit, and they think it is another entity. They even give it a name. And yet it is only the light of their own beings they are seeing, because your light will often focus in front of you and you'll get glimmers of it. That light is where you get all of your answers, for it is connected to the Mind of God. So, rather than calling it Chief Redfeather, or Dr. Ming Hing Poo of the Third Dynasty, or George, call it what it is: I AM! It *does* know *everything*.

Now, many of you have heard a voice in your head, and you have immediately thought that you're a channel or a medium. You are not. Why can't you accept that it is your *own* knowingness, because *that* indeed is what you are hearing.

Stars and planets do not govern your life, for no thing outside of you governs you unless you allow it to. It is a hypocrisy to say that *you* are God, and then say that the *universe* has planned your destiny! Know you why astrology works? Because entities *believe* it into working; their thoughts are *that* powerful! And yet they give credit to the stars.

You have entities tell you what *you* know, and then you give *them* all the credit! You are giving your power away to them, to the stars! to crystals! to teachers! *Wake up!* No wonder the gurus have had a field day in your country! *(Shakes his head)* No wonder!

When you ask yourself, the god of your being, it *knows*; it has the answers. When you ask someone else, it's always a fruitless game, a riddle, a speculation.

These are all spiritual dogmas. And it's all right to believe in them if that's your truth. But dogma is a hypocrisy to divine inner revelation. As long as you believe in a power outside of you, you'll never become God. Never!

Now you understand why so many entities do not love me—because I kick away their crutches. *(Picks up his glass, sighs, and toasts the audience)* To the human comedy.

Now, another spiritual dogma. Know you "The Path"? In religion it is so narrow (because narrow-minded entities created it), not everybody can get on it!

The path to enlightenment is not *one* path. The path is right wherever you are.

Do you know that your path can wind, go over hills, through dales and glens, pass through sleepy hollows, cross rivers and babbling brooks? Know you that it can go under the sea, over the sea, or perhaps to the other side of the moon? How will you know if you are on the right path? When you've got a smile on your face; when what you're doing makes you *happy*. The right path is wherever you are happy.

Now, if your path has a fork in the road and you have an option, and neither one makes you happy, and you're confused, do not make a decision. Do not! Never make a decision when you are confused. Allow the answer to come. It won't take a century, only moments. Stand there with a smile on your face, right where you are, and allow the confusion to subside. When you *allow* it, the path will become clear, because it will *feel* good. It may not be right for others, but it will be for you. Happiness is the only path to enlightenment, because the more you are gratifying yourself and living in a state of joy, the closer you are to God, for joy *is* what the Father is.

Know you what boredom is? It is your soul telling you that you have learned everything from that experience. The experience no longer intrigues you, challenges you, or uplifts you, because you already learned what you wanted to learn from it. If you are bored with something, it's time to change; it's time to move on. This is applicable to labor, creativity, relationships, husbands, wives, lovers. It applies to everything! A master knows when he has gained all there is to gain, and he moves on. And he goes only in the directions that bring him happiness and joy. Of course, you can live in the same hovel for the rest of your life. If you are completely happy there, stay there. But let your soul speak to you and tell you where your happiness lies.

Now, what is the voice of God? What is that knowingness you thought would come from the heavens like a bolt of lightning and tell you what to do? It is *feelings*. To hear the voice of God is to listen to what you *feel*. Feelings are, indeed, the unspeakable knowledge. Now you know why I cannot teach you that knowingness—because *you* must feel it! I can *tell* you of that feeling, but you'll never understand what I am talking about until *you* experience it.

(Toasts the audience) To boredom! To change! To the future! Forever and ever and ever! So be it!

Audience: (Toasting with him) So be it!

Ramtha: Now, get happy! Get rid of the things in your life that do not bring you joy. You *know* what they are. All you have to do is look around you. Look at your walls. What do you hang there? What do you read? What enslaves you? What limits you? No matter what it is, allow it to flow from your life. *Anything that doesn't bring you joy, get rid of it!* It's liken unto a leech! If you are not happy in your relationship, say so. Be honorable; live your truth. For the first time, *live your truth*. If you want to move, move! What is stopping you?

Don't do anything that doesn't bring you joy. If you do, that is not loving you. Be fair with yourself. Do what brings you joy, in spite of everyone else. Do it for the sake of God within you and go for it!

You have been given grand teachings, and I have hard-pressed them to you. You will be even more hard-pressed when you leave this audience. You will be pressed into your masterhood—because you *want* to be! The knowingness that would have taken you lifetimes to gain, you are gaining in moments. I salute you for allowing that to occur. So be it! That is all.

***

21

The Days To Come

Know you what Nature is? It is the wondrous continuum of birthing, called Forever. Nature—the earth, the sun, the beauty of the enchantress moon, the forever stars, the wind upon the water, the seasons—*is* reality. It is the wondrous platform upon which you live out your illusions. It is Nature who, through photosynthesis in your plant life, allows all your dreams to manifest upon this plane.

Many have spiritualized Nature into being; many have rationalized it into being. Well, both are right. Nature is God, or Thought, realizing itself in *all* of its forms. It is God, or Life, *evolving*. When Thought contemplated itself, evolution was born; and that inevitable cycle will continue forever—in *spite* of you.

So, Nature, the immutable law of God in its adventure into itself, is evolving. It is not changeable by man. And if you try to war with Nature, it shall always be victorious over you.

Now, let us talk about your sun, for it has a profound effect upon you and your earth. You are in a *tenuous balance* with its life, yet few of you realize this.

Your sun, in its core, is Thought reflecting into itself; that is what creates the light. The light creates fission, and the fission

Excerpted and edited from *Ramtha Intensive: Change, The Days To Come*, which presents an edited transcription of a two-day teaching held in May, 1986, along with related material presented in 1986 and 1987.

creates the fire, the raw birthing energy. The winds that pre-
vail around the sun's grandiose light are called winds of the
solar system, and they carry light particums not only to your
earth, but to the farthest planet in your solar system. The light
particums and the solar winds control your weather.

Heard you of the term "sun spot"? Know you what that is?
It is simply your sun *evolving*, becoming more and more. It is
the explosion of Thought occurring. Every moment that eruption occurs and reaches *millions* of miles into the universe,
you are seeing *creation*; you are seeing Thought coming into
the fission of the X and Y particums to create matter. And during an eruption of "Thought becoming matter," the solar
winds that control your weather are at hurricane gusts.

Your sun is becoming spotted; it is fixing to have a belly-
ache. And these eruptions are going to have a lot to do with
you, who are of *tenuous* flesh and blood. Your weather conditions are already beginning to reflect the thought that is manifesting as a great spot upon your sun. Already your weather
has become erratic and unpredictable. All you have to do is
look and you will know that changes are coming in Nature.
They are part of a *natural* cycle of evolution that is working *in
harmony* with your earth plane.

By the end of this decade, you are going to see a *huge* spot
on your sun, with flares the likes of which your scientists have
never seen before. With it comes drastic weather changes that
will profoundly affect you who are *unprepared* for it.

Now, you must understand something about Nature and its
cycles of change. Change is purposeful ev-o-lu-tion, the
ripening expansion of Life. And in each new moment of its
expansion, Life will be grander and grander. Change is to
move *forward* into today and that which is called tomorrow.
Change is the basis of demonstrated forever, and it will continue on and on and on, for it is God in its immutable law
called Nature.

Now, your sun isn't spotting because it's ticked off at you.
It is simply in its *natural* cycle of expansion; as a result, your

earth plane is going to *react* to that evolutionary process.

What is coming upon your plane is a drought. We are talking about *thirsty soil*, soil lacking the nourishment that allows wheat to expand from a seed to the full birthing of its beautiful, golden stalks.

Know you when you are hungry for dinner, and it has always been so *convenient* to drive and pick up foodstuffs? You never think about where your food comes from, because you can always run hurry-scurry to the market and *squeeze* that bread! Fresh! Fresh! Fresh! So, you don't think about Nature. You don't realize and appreciate this grand, fundamental reality. You are too caught up in the convenience you have created, and you have become lazy entities who are going to be *unprepared*. You have wrapped yourselves up in your own illusions, your own problems, and you concern yourselves with *petty* things. You are oblivious to what's going on under your feet and in your heavens. You are limited people because your vision has become very constricted.

Soon, you are going to be besieged upon the land because there will be no water. Your Bread Basket is going to become depleted. Your abundance will go very rapidly because you are feeding everyone else in the world.

Nature, the evolutionary process, is in harmony with *everything* except you who are terrified because you cannot *imagine* living off the land, because you are used to driving to your super-super-super-supermarkets and picking something up.

Masters, so you know what I am telling you is a truth, get out of your petty little boxes and go do research at your libraries. Talk with your scientists. Do it! Then you will understand that this knowingness has now reached many of your people, who are also endeavoring to communicate this truth to you.

Now, understand this: The time of the drought *can* change. It can be at a later time. But it *is* coming; it is already effective. This is not something to be angry about; it is simply Nature evolving. But perhaps, masters, you should look at your cupboards and assess how in harmony you are with Nature and its changes. If you are in harmony with it, you understand its cycles, you embrace that knowledge, and you are prepared. If you are not in harmony with Nature, you will scuttle about wondering why God has brought this plague on you (which is your natural reaction—to blame everyone else except yourself). Well, you can squiggle and cry all you want to, but it will do no good.

This drought is one thing that is coming in the days to come, but it is only a *small* part of what is coming. We have not yet talked about what *you* have created and its effects on your days to come. We are talking first of Nature, because without Nature you will *have* no days to come!*

Now, you have been looking for "divine" inspiration. You have been burning incense, chanting, deciphering your dreams and visions, reading the leaves in teacups. You've been running to teachers, consulting guides, asking those who have set themselves up as "knowing entities" all about those small things, like: "What of my relationship?" "What of my career?" "Can you change so-and-so's mind about me?" And they're glad to give you answers; all you have to do is ask. And if you ask ten thousand people, you will have ten thousand *different* answers!

You have been looking for *the* truth. Well, the truth *is*, you've been looking in the wrong places! Because where are your teachers and guides going to be when you're *hungry*? Hmm? They may give you food for *thought*, but that really isn't going to cut it when the drought comes.

Now, one of the grandest teachers of all is the ant—you know, those pesty little creatures that are intent upon snatching away the deli from your picnic or the crumbs you carelessly left in your kitchen. In my days, I watched ants with great love and respect, and I saw such a grand *intelligence* from such a minute, determined entity. If they were people,

---

*In the full text of the teaching, Ramtha discussed many other changes that are coming in Nature and world conditions.

they would have all become God and ascended long ago, because *they* don't have any hang-ups!

Now, we are talking of teachers in Nature; we are talking about the *real* thing. These entities are delighted when the glow of a spring sun begins to melt the winter snow. They become very busy excavating themselves right out of their hovels to bask in the wonderful warmth, in the rejuvenation of another spring to be lived. Straightaway, these wondrous creatures begin cleaning out their closets, so to speak, and then they begin their collection of foodstuffs. And they work *in harmony*.

Masters, if you put a town of people and an antbed side by side, *which* do you think would work together most harmoniously? I assure you, the ants would. In the town, there would be cursing and fistfights breaking out, because you have proven through your times that you can't work together. Well, you'll soon have the chance to change this.

The ants labor, play, and are joyful. They store food all spring, summer and fall, for they certainly know that the great white silence will return to the land. They prepare for it. They do not do it out of fear, but out of a natural desire to survive. They do not *hate* the winter; they *understand* the winter, and they know how long it will last. When spring comes again, they will have survived it all—and they *know* that spring *always* follows winter. In their knowingness, the ants are fully aware of the sun and the earth in their evolutionary processes. They are great teachers for you. Yet how could you ever bring yourselves down to an ant's level, when you are endeavoring *so* arduously to become *so* exalted!

Now, for the lot of you, I will send you some runners, and the runners will be ants. And you will find them in the most *unexpected* places. If you spray the little devils into oblivion, you will have just slaughtered your great teachers!

I desire for you to watch what they're doing. If you say, "Oh, I won't do that!" I'll send them to you *one thousand-fold*. So, you won't be able to *help* but watch. I do this because I love you.

Observe them. I know you are larger than they, but they are swifter, more clever, and more determined than most of you. Perhaps, in observing them with great humility, you will gain the virtue of *their* noble attitudes and allow them to teach you something, emotionally, about being prepared.

Now, how much food do you have in your pantries? How long will it last? Two days? Three weeks? If you do not have enough provisions for *two years*, you are going to run perilously short. Sun spots have caused droughts that have, for the most part, lasted for at least two years in counting.

To prepare yourselves in this way is not adding to fear in social consciousness. The ant does not add to fear. It adds to the *harmony* of Nature because it *is* in harmony; it is in alignment with what it *knows* to be a truth.

Surviving need *not* be a hardship. When you are in flow with Nature, you never have to *struggle* to survive, because you are just "in the flow." If you are scrambling to find shelter and something to eat, you are at a place of *base* survival. You are working *against* the flow, because you have not been in harmony with the movement, the cycles of Nature.

Is this a fearsome truth? Is it "doom and gloom"? How could *Nature* be doom and gloom? How could it be anything but admirably *beautiful*? But if you fight it, if you are against it, you will not win, because Nature *knows* it is forever, while you are still tenuous.

To prepare is not foolish, it is a *wise* thing to do. If an entity has even a small piece of land, he can grow his staff of life, and he can preserve that which he grows. That will carry him through even the most arduous of circumstances. Then he is free. But *you* are *not* free! When your drought comes and the baker doesn't bake the bread because the wheat isn't there, because the wheat didn't grow, because the rains weren't there, how are you going to have bread? Do you even know how to bake it? Do you know how to grow wheat and glean it from the chaff? You *don't* know, because are no longer in love with the land, only with *convenience*, which says a lot about what you think of time.

Know you, masters, who will inherit the earth? Know you who will inherit the kingdom of heaven and the new understanding that I term Superconsciousness? It is not the intellectual! It is not those who worship complexities! It is the *meek*, those who are *humble* within their beings, who are close to the earth and work *harmoniously* with it, who are in *alignment* with it. And they do not *play* with the illusion of death.

Many of you are vacillating between your desire for enlightenment and your fantasies of death and dying and suicide. Well, you will have the chance to choose. You will find your fantasies fleeing from your being, because a nature within you will surface; it is called the desire for *survival*.

The meek are *always* prepared. They store up provisions, not because they are anticipating a great calamity, but because they love themselves and others enough to always be sovereign and never be at the mercy of *anyone* else.

You are not free people! You *think* you are, but that is your illusion in your little boxes. You know your box? Tidy, immaculate, scrubbed, no odors.

How free *are* you? If it ever happened that there was no food in the markets of your cities (and it is going to), who are you at the mercy of? If you have not grown or bought sufficient food, what sort of freedom do you have? Who is going to give you a handout?

Nature is the wild, *free*, ever-moving life-force. On this plane, only Nature exhibits complete freedom. You exhibit complete enslavement, because you depend upon things *outside* of you.

You can reconcile this knowingness any way you want to. You can make all the excuses you want. You can find all the reasons why this *shouldn't* be a truth. That is all right. But those who know it is a truth, *know*—because they listen to their god speaking within them. They *feel* it! They are feeling

Nature. They are watching the weather. They are walking out into the wind. No one has to *tell* them; they just know, and they live in harmony with their knowingness. Because of that, they will see Superconsciousness. That is simply how it is.

Now, your cities are seductresses. They are desirous of everyone to be there, yet they love none who are. What would you reason about your cities in the days to come? Contemplate this with common, *simple* reasoning. Why are they not advantageous places to be in the days to come? Reason it! *No fields.* All turnpikes. There are hovels on top of one another, and the only thing that grows there are baskets of flowers.

Where does their food come from? Where does their water come from? Reason this out; then you will understand why the city is not an advantageous place to be. And the cities are going to be the first to spew forth the diseases and the plagues that are coming—indeed, are already here. This is not ominous. It is simple knowingness and simple reasoning.

The days to come are loaded with many surprises, but they are surprises only for the *un*knowing, the *un*prepared, the ones who do not want to listen because it is too big of a deal to do anything about this knowingness.

Where will you get two years' worth of foodstuffs? Well, you have bountiful markets, don't you? Be bountiful in your acquisition from them. You have wonderful ways to preserve things. Go and secure however much you want. You will know when it is enough. And put it away in a clean, *clean* place.

What of your water? If you are living in the city, you are in for *big* trouble. If you are living on the simple earth, find your water, drill a well, and *have it there*. Make your wells so that water is always accessible to you.

Now, know you what electrum is? It is Light that has been lowered into an electrical field of negative/positive energy. That is what creates the electricity that you plug into. Know you what it is to "plug in"? How many moments only this morning did you plug in? Hmm? If your electricity wasn't there, many of you wouldn't have any curls on top of your head. And many of you would not have clean teeth, because if you couldn't plug in, it just wouldn't happen. Reason that for a moment.

Electrum is a wild force that is *everywhere*. A brilliant, *simple* entity with vision and foresight discovered the way to harness it. Unfortunately, you have given up your sovereignty because you have become dependent upon it for your survival and enjoyment.

In Nature, electrum is an energy that is prevalent everywhere. There will come a day, very shortly, when all you will need is a lightning rod to harness the magnetic energy of your northern and southern regions. You won't need to "plug in" at all. This will allow you to be even more sovereign. The meek will be the first to know about this, because they are *simple* enough to *reason* it.

Now, I am giving you an educational process of common reasoning to encourage you to use your common sense, which *is* simplicity. To learn and embrace the physics of defined Nature is a grand and enlightened thing to do. To understand your plane is utterly important in the process of becoming God, because you do not become God *without* this plane. You cannot learn these things through chants; they are a no thing. Rituals are a no thing. Your guides and teachers are a no thing, because they are *not* going to walk in your shoes.

Enlightenment means "to be in knowledge of." To be God is not to be a cloistered, superficial, dogmatic entity. That is to die! To become enlightened is to embrace *knowledge*, to wake up to a grander understanding that encompasses *all life*. To be enlightened means that you *know*, because with knowingness, you have absolute freedom and can make any move.

Do you *know*, masters, that you are doing away with oxygen in your stratum? And since you're breathing animals, what are you going to breathe? Do you know you are poisoning your environment? *(Audience members nod.)* You *do* know that. Then *why* are you plugging into an energy source that is now threatening Europa and parts of the Ukraine? *(referring to the aftermath of the Chernobyl accident)* To know . . . is to *do*. If you *know* these things, *why haven't you changed them*? When one becomes truly "in knowledge of," he is *spurred* to change. You cannot say you know these things without changing them. Understand?

Masters, *you* have created the things that are destroying your very existence here; Nature is simply responding. You say, "How could I have been a part of the reactor accident at Chernobyl?" You have pity for the poor entities who are suffering there, but you think you didn't have anything to do with that because it happened in another country. The truth is, you had *everything* to do with it, because you have not *allowed* your mind to wake up and become inventive and sovereign. Your political governments still have to rely on energy that is perilous to the human cell in order to keep you plugged in. Get it? Own it, because it is a great truth.

Where are your *windmills*? Where are your *solar energy systems*? You think you are enlightened entities, but where is your mind? Where is your motivation? *Where*, god, is your *sovereignty*?

You have added to your world's energy problems, and you will add to all its other problems unless you create the attitude to change how you live, to manifest wisdom into action. Whatever you do is based on what you think; and whatever you are thinking is being fed back into the consciousness that feeds the thinking of everyone all over your world. It only takes one entity to establish self-ordained sovereignty to affect the entire world. For the feeling of that freedom, which allows one to sleep restful nights, goes out into social consciousness for someone else to pick up. That is how you become a "living light to the world."

If you are in harmony with Nature, you are *sovereign* with it. Then Nature will feed you. It will supply you with your electrical needs. It will supply you with your transport needs. It will build your hovels. And wherever you poke a hole in the ground, it will give you fresh water.

Love of self is not a nine-to-five job. It is the harmonious movement of oneself in alignment with God, which is Nature. *That* is loving oneself.

Is it an accursed thing to have your larder filled? Is it an accursed thing to sit down to a meager meal and know your energy produced it, to know you gave it life? Because it is thus, it will taste better and be much more nutritious than anything you have ever purchased from any market.

What do you find dreadful about being prepared? The ant is perpetual in its preparation *every year* that the seasons pass. Know you that in your great ice age, they survived? Know you that every animal life that had the qualities of hibernation and preparation survived to carry on? I am speaking to you of *purposeful sovereignty*. For I assure you, you are hard-pressed when you have become a beggar who must plead for shelter and bread. One should never live like that. One should live in complete freedom, not austerity.

I *love* you, but I see how unprepared you are for *everything*, because you've been looking in directions that can do nothing for you. I see your desire to know, but unless you are prepared, you are not going to survive. Though you may think this teaching is a lark, when the sun begins to spot itself, who are you going to borrow a biscuit from? Those of you who insist upon living in a city because it is close to work, ask yourself if it is worth it.

You are God. *(Shouts)* You are God! And you say, "Big deal. How is it going to up my salary? How is it going to secure my mortgage? How is it going to help my relationship?" This that you are learning about is called Life. All of these other things have to surrender to this knowledge. If they don't, you will have no life to wonder about.

It is inherently within you to survive, even as lazy as you've become. "Why, the very thought of plowing the fields again and milking a cow! Really!" Well, you need to be revived in spirit and in soul. That occurs when you come out of your illusions and become the sovereign entities you truly are. If it takes planting your own food to become that, then do it. If it takes drilling your own well, do it! And if Nature, in all her splendor, decides not to expand her glowing self and create sunspots, what you will have done is still *wonderful*. Your sovereignty in Nature would allow common sense to be sown in your direful social consciousness. It would allow mankind to grow into their divinity, to come full-circle: from sovereign gods who made their advent onto this plane, to limited man, to man waking up to *total sovereignty*.

This that you are learning, *do* something with it! The changes in Nature are already happening. Take the knowingness and the knowledge I have given you, and *feel what you feel*, and *move* according to that emotion. The god within you will take you where you need to go.

Learn to be sovereign. Learn to be prepared. Find a place where you feel one with life, and go forward. If you don't want to do that because it's too much of a problem, so be it; you're still loved. But now you know.

Now, the human race has been working up to an explosive state. Nations are vying to be the ultimate power. You have a great conflict between religion and government; you have a great conflict for allegiance. You have separated yourselves from your brothers, and, as a result, you have to post guards and create arms to protect your borders, your homes, and your children.

How have *you* added to all of this? Through your attitude—by thinking everyone is your enemy, when your real enemy is your *own perception*.

Everything you think affects all entities around the world, for it adds to the social structure of thought. And whatever you fear, you draw to yourself. You create the aura of suspicion and then draw to you those who are suspicious.

All of you nod your heads and smile about the brotherhood of people everywhere. You *talk* about loving all people, but *do you*? Do you *love* your neighbor? Do you love your family, without terms?

Know you war? You *should*; you do it *every day*. You do it whenever you argue your truth with someone else and tell them that they're wrong and you're right. That, indeed, is war. War doesn't have to be on a battlefield; it can be in your own backyard or in your own bathroom.

I have watched you judge others for their beliefs, their political stands, for the way they look or don't look. Whenever you judge *anyone*, you judge *the whole of the world*! And what is that creating out in your world? It is creating the separation of brother from brother. It is creating *hatred*. It is creating insecurity in others, who become so fearful that they will seek to destroy you.

What is worth judging? Who is not worth *allowing*. Hmm? Can't you allow them the mercy and freedom to be their own selves? If you are bent on changing a person, you must assess whether you truly believe in your *own* ideals. When you try to convert someone to your truth, it means you're not convinced of what you "know," and you're looking for support in numbers. Did you know that?

It is not someone else's fault that the world is in the state it's in. Through your attitude, you have contributed to the dissension in your streets, you have created your terrorists and your mad rulers, you have created bitterness toward you from those abroad. All of you have! Own up to it, because you have added to all of it by how you think. Your attitudes toward yourself and toward others in your own small world has added to the misery of the whole. Your world condition isn't just there! Your attitude and the attitude of every other entity creates and supports it.

Masters, *everyone* is God—however they are expressing, however they look, wherever they live. Whether or not they accept that truth, they are *still* God and they are loved as such.

There are people in your country who want to destroy the people of the Land of the Bear and the people of yellow skin because they don't believe in God. They are going to *destroy*

them because they don't believe in God? It isn't important
whether or how one believes in God! Whatever they believe,
they are divine, because they live and breathe, they contemplate and doubt, and they are fearful, *just like you*!

Divine intervention is occurring upon this plane, because
what has been created here is the threat of annihilation. Why
do you think your rockets are falling from the heavens? You
think these are simply malfunctions? Why do you think that
your surveillance systems are being destroyed? Because your
country, the Country of the Bear, and other countries are not
up in space for scientific reasons. They are there to thrust
themselves like eagles and make their nests among the stars in
order to have dominion over heaven and earth. That is the desire of the warlords who lead your country and all other countries. After all, one who could sit at the pinnacle of a sunrise,
who could hang on the silvery moon, would certainly have dominion over the rest of you. If that were to happen, what
would you do? Spit at him?

Your attitude of pushing your philosophies and governments on other entities is coming to a close. That is much
needed after seven and one-half million years of giving away
your power and then struggling to get it back. There is so
much that Nature is going to be enacting, that very few
entities are going to have time to think about war. Man's mind
is going to be taken off his distrust of his neighbor and his su-
perior attitude toward others. He is going to be faced with survival, *base* survival, where hunger is all he can think about.
That will build character and allow him the humility to see the
vanity of war and conquering and borders and mistrust. If it
takes *that* to bring the world to a *common* pursuit, a *common*
link, it will indeed be worth it.

No bombs are ever going to destroy your country or the
Country of the Bear. *That will never happen*. The warlords are
dying; their thunder is being taken away. The time is over for
those who breed the annihilation of the people of this plane.

You will not know war in this country, not on a cataclysmic

scale. But you are going to learn to know *yourself* through Nature and its changes. You are going to learn what it is to be God in its most sovereign sense.

It is utterly up to you to create your destiny through the attitude of *self*-destiny. This is important for the *whole* of mankind, in all places. You are approaching the time when this is going to be necessary for the survival of these entities who are gods asleep in the dream called mankind. All people need to reassess the seeds of their virtue. This is already happening.

In the days to come, you will see many changes in your systems, your governments, and your thinking. Each will scale another rung on the ladder toward the freedom of all people. Coming to the surface, day by day, moment by moment, are *meek people* who, in the sincerity of their beings, have found peace with the whole of the world. Collectively, the meek all over the world are casting the shadow of the days to come, of a grander world, a loving one that God certainly is the manifesting force behind.

Many of you shall never live to see Superconsciousness on this plane. Why? Look at what you are doing. Look at how you are living. Many of you will perish in the days to come because you will not *change* your attitudes; you will not let go of your beliefs, dogmas, bigotries, prejudices, insecurities, and guilts. You will not see Superconsciousness because you have not humbled your pride to allow yourselves to see it. If you choose to hold on to things of no importance, and you do not prepare and take care of yourselves through the humility of meekness, you will perish in the days to come. That is all right. Death is not an ominous thing. Choosing whatever you want to do is your right. But know that you are choosing, and take full responsibility for that. You are loved *regardless* of what you do. You have *always* been loved regardless of what you do. You cannot fathom how well you have been taken care of to keep you from destroying yourselves.

The days that are coming are the days of black and white. One will either be in the throes of change, creating right within himself, or he will die with the old. That is how it is. These are not the days for those who walk the middle of the road. These are the days for those who are *doing*.

Nature will continue to change in spite of you. *Your* territory for change is *your attitude*, and that is within your own dominion. And what you change affects the whole. That is how *you* make a difference. Whether you are going to go back to sleep or whether you are going to live and profoundly affect the *whole* of humanity is up to you.

(Looks tenderly at the audience) I love you. There is *illuminated* divinity in your beings. Each of you is grander and more dear to me than you can fathom. I love to walk with you, to be in your slumber, to look into your eyes, to touch your delicate hair and skin, and connect with your souls. To me, though you are vast in numbers, each of you is unique and grand and God.

You do not realize through what time barriers and dimensions this miracle has occurred. Though you take it for granted, contemplate for a moment what mastery and power it has taken to be here with you, on common ground, utilizing your *outrageous* common speech. I have expedited your time in order to be with you, to walk with you, to talk with you, and to allow the feelings to come forward.

You are my brothers. Once, many of you lived in my army. You are the reason I have come back here for a sojourn. I am waiting for the hour when you remember who you are. In great repetition, I have taught you a simple, *simple* truth, waiting for you to wake up. You are the hope of the world. You don't know that, but you are.

Where is one who can embrace the whole of the world and love all people regardless of their faith, their political ideals, or their past? Where is one who can love them and *allow* them to be? Through allowing, one nurtures, unequivocally, peace. When there's peace, there is joy; and when there is joy, there is God, remembered and embraced.

The days to come are riddled with changes that will affect

all of you. But far greater than what the future holds is where you are in your discovery of yourselves. The purpose of this teaching is not only to prepare you for the days to come; it is to plant the seeds of discovery within you and help you ripen. These days, and the things that are at hand, are only the backdrop of the stage upon which you are going to finish your act. When one by one you begin to wake up, and you realize, embrace, and know what you are, then you are as free as the wind, and you will bring to the world its greatest hope and its greatest revelation.

This is not, as you term it, a "pep talk." It is the most profound truth of all. Your adventures in discovery have little to do with technology; they have everything to do with going within and discovering the unexplored regions of your identity. To do this, you must peel away, *one by one*, the limitations, the clouds, the layers of your limited identity—by *humbling* yourselves to do it—until you find the light within and hear the voice that speaks to you in tranquil, sublime emotion. It is God! When you have reached that, you have come home.

Now, I have not told you of all the things that are going to come to pass. It is not that I hold out on you, but you have had enough of what has been given to you in bell-ringing clarity. Fortified with this wisdom, you can withstand everything. I assure you, the days to come will indeed be ominous to many people. But be jubilant, for it is *not* ominous; it is the grand adventure of a new world, a new consciousness, a new understanding, and peace. It is worth weathering anything to see Superconsciousness. The understanding I have brought you, I have spoken evenly and clearly. If you did not hear it, it is by your choice. I respect your will and still love you in your decision.

Go wherever it *feels* right. Do whatever feels right, what rings in your soul. Be in a state of awareness and *trust* what you feel. Live *your* truth. It may not be the truth of your family or your friends, but that does not mean you're in error. Nor

does it mean *they* are in error. It simply means that you are
honoring what you feel.

Be at peace with yourself and what you are doing and feeling. Understand that you are doing these things for the Father
within you, and that you are in the process of waking up. Do
not, I beseech you, be intimidated out of your knowingness. It
will be *easy* for you to give it away again and go back to sleep
when someone says, "You are *all wrong!*" You're *never*
wrong when something *feels* right. Never!

Now, masters, that which I am, termed Ramtha the Enlightened One, has become controversial. To many, what I teach is
very threatening, and I understand that.

This teaching, this understanding, is going to many places,
indeed. It is reaching like great arms over vast distances, over
wide seas, to many people. In the days to come, you are going
to hear my name spoken over and over and over. For many of
you, what will be spoken of me and of what I teach will break
your hearts. And many of you will rejoice, for you will see
that people from all over your world are coming to these understandings.

But masters, hear what I have to say unto all of you. *Do not
march on my behalf.* What others are to know of me, is for
them to learn. You do not have to defend me or yourself.
Simply go about your lives and live what I have taught you,
for you have never learned anything so great as you have
learned from these teachings.

Joy, what is it? It is a feeling that is thrilling, electrifying,
all-encompassing. It is happiness, it is dreams fulfilled. I have
been teaching you, eloquently, to find that joy. But if ever
what I am causes conflict within your life, I desire that you not
acknowledge me. I wish never to stand in the way of the experiences you are needing for your fulfillment.

Many will have an arduous time accepting or understanding
that which I am and the teachings I give forth, for they have
yet to open up their thought processes to allow the wonderment of their minds to be born. That is all right. They are still

loved by me and the Father within them. But I say unto you, do not become embattled or allow yourselves to be ridiculed or tormented because of who I am. I am not a cause to be fought for. I am an isness that is and always will be. Never be persecuted for me. Never fight because of me. Any moment you pick up the sword, you have already lost. I know. I carried one for a long time.

Be an example of what I have taught you and *live* these teachings. Love who you are. Embrace joy and happiness. Experience life. Love all people.

If you are needing a confidant, all you have to do is speak to me. I will press to you love and understanding, but only to teach you how to give these to yourself. And if anyone wishes to lay hold on you because of what you have heard from me, deny me *completely*—but remember what I taught you! *(Softly)* Because it is all true.

(Raises his glass and toasts) To knowingness and the Father within, forever and ever and ever. So be it!

Audience: So be it!

Ramtha: Now, I have many audiences coming forward. And you wonder, "Which one do I go to?" I did not create these audiences so that you need to go to every one of them! These audiences are wisdom given forth so that you may open up your eyes again and go home. There *is* coming the day when you will have awakened and owned it all, because you will have realized that you have created it all; you will have realized how *powerful* you are. Then, what else needs to be said? Hmm? I will have come and been a mirror to my people. One day there will be no longer be the need for a mirror. And what awaits is a vastness of unexplored life that is your kingdom of heaven. One by one, you'll come home to where be I—and *that* is an adventure in itself. Until that hour comes, I will be here to teach and to challenge your closed minds to wake up. Whatever it takes, I will do it, because you have desired it.

Wherever you go upon this plane, and whatever you do, I

will always be the wind that is around you. For those of you who take this truth and this knowingness into your souls, and release that which limits the grandness of your becoming, you will see the days to come. A grand wind will carry you there.

Go and be happy, wherever that is. So be it.

***

22

The Fallible Dream

Ramtha: (Addressing an audience on the topic "Financial Freedom") So, you're all here after money! *(Audience laughs and applauds)*

In my innocence, I have asked those who have come into my audience, "What desire you, master?" And they would say to me, "Ramtha, I desire to be God." And *then* they would say, "And I also want to be rich!" So I am cutting through all of that. You're all here to learn how to get more money, what I term "gold."

Now, gold is a tender, shiny metal that has always had value on your plane, for it is rare and of great beauty. It is a soft, sensitive metal that is the greatest of all metals, because it absorbs emotional frequencies. Put on the gold breastplate of a king, and within moments you will feel his preeminence, his glory in wearing it, because his emotion is locked into the metal. In other words, gold is liken unto the soul, for it holds emotions.

Many of you in this audience feel that every one of your problems would be taken care of if you just had enough... *(waiting for audience to complete sentence)* Well, speak up, hypocrites!

Audience: (Laughing) Money!

Ramtha: Indeed. Many of you think that money, or gold, is the answer to all your prayers. Everything revolves around it,

---

Excerpted and edited from *Ramtha Intensive: Change, The Days To Come.*

and that is what you dream about and envision yourself having. So how do I teach you that it is far greater to replace the desire for gold with the desire for *genius*, the mind that can create it all?

I am telling all of you this for a reason. If all you dream about is having more money, you are in for a rude awakening, because your world is on the brink of bankruptcy. Even your nation has a greater deficit than you know.

Listen to me, masters. Your paper money is not *your* money! It is not owned by your country. It is owned by the Federal Reserve, which is owned by *international* bankers composed of the most powerful families since the hour of Napoleon. I was amazed to see how many of you think that because it says "Federal," it means your government owns it. Well, it doesn't. The Federal Reserve is owned by a few families who have no allegiance to any country or to any people. Their allegiance is only to power and wealth. These entities even create wars to gain power and to control the destiny of mankind.

Do you know that your country does not go to war because of a noble virtue! It goes to war because it's *good business*! You don't know that, eh?

Now, your country no longer has the gold to back up its paper money. And when gold no longer backs up your money, you are treading on thin ice, because then these entities can dictate how much, or how little, your dollars are worth. Then you are . . . *(holds out his hands)*

Audience Member: Wiped out!

Ramtha: Wiped out? Hungry! Wanting. Needing. Unhappy.

It is not *you* who create inflation and deflation; it is not *you* who create rises and falls in the price of your stocks and bonds. That is all an illusion. International powers, the ones who own all the money, sit around your wondrous globe like players in a chess game, and they pull all the strings.

Now, there is a conspiracy of sorts to break the backbone of your middle class so that there is wealth for only a very few, who will govern all of the "rabble" —you! Why does this situation exist? Because these entities are gods, just as you are, and they are playing out *their* dream; it is what they are needing for *their* learning. Well, that is all right; their hour is coming to an end.

Now that you are *aware* of the situation, begin to assess what you really want, and whether you desire a dream that is not so fallible. In other words, isn't it far greater to be able to manifest what money can buy, rather than the money to buy it? When you learn to embrace the feeling of what you want the money to purchase, you'll get it, lickety split.

So here we have you who are blatantly ignorant about how your economic system works, who are very naive about power. And here we have you who have spit in my eye when I said, "Put away food," because you want what "really" counts. Well, one day, grasshopper, you'll be sitting outside the ant's door, knocking.

***

23

The Most
Alien Entity

Master: Ramtha, recently there seems to be an increase in the number of UFO sightings and abductions by aliens. Also, there seems to be an increase in the number of people channeling extraterrestrial beings. I was wondering if there is anything you might like—

Ramtha: (After roaring with laughter) A new dogma, eh?

Master: I'm not sure what you mean. But I know a lot of people are interested in this. I was wondering if these extraterrestrials are just watching us, or are they planning to help us through the days to come?

Ramtha: Help you? Why do you think you need help?

Master: To get beyond social consciousness, I guess.

Ramtha: Master, know you the term "spinning your wheels"? As if things weren't troublesome enough, now you are concerned about aliens sitting up in spaceships somewhere; and you're wondering whether they are going to intervene and save your skin. And if they *are* coming, you're *hoping* that you'll be in the right place at the right time to be picked up. Correct?

Master: Well . . .

Ramtha: Let me give you a truth. If you don't like it, or if you choose to have a different one, then by all means go for it!

Excerpted and edited from *Ramtha Intensive: Change, The Days To Come*.

The entities in these ships are your higher brothers. Now, by "higher," I do not mean they are *greater* than you; they are just high up in the sky somewhere, that is all. These "aliens," as they are termed, do exist, and they do come here. They come from other solar systems, other dimensions, and even from the center of your earth. Though many of them have looks that differ greatly from yours, that you would term ugly because you judge beauty to be the outward dimension, they are beauteous entities, indeed.

These entities are your brothers, not your *saviors*, yet they are being worshiped on a massive scale here because of the many myths that surround them. To think that one of them is speaking through you is most glorious, but it is also hogwash! If you really want to channel an intelligent mind, try channeling an ant! They have a better understanding of what is going to happen, how to get things organized, and where to dig in, than any other creature.

Master, unless something can put bread on your table or challenge your mind into living *here-and-now*, into living in joy and becoming sovereign, it's of no importance. It is just another idol, another game, another illusion. There are many things I *could* teach you, and many wonderful adventures you could go on, but mankind is not ready for them. For he hasn't unglued himself from the bonds of idol worship, and he hasn't released himself from the glamour and excitement of fear. He gets off the track by always looking to things "out there" instead of taking a hard look at what's inside.

When you get beyond the need to look outside yourself, you will find peace and alignment with all things. Then you will know of *every* wonderful thing that exists. And you won't know of them *second hand*, because then you will be in the flow of all life.

Knowledge, reasoning, knowing that God is within you and touching the hem of that divinity—that is your only salvation.

There are so many things you utterly take for granted. If you spin your wheels in search of bright lights in the sky, you are never going to appreciate the beauty of the earth you are standing upon, or the beauty of the one who is searching for them. It is a wise and prudent entity who undertakes the discovery of *self* and his *own* environment before he casts his eyes to the "beyond" into forever. Only when man accepts and owns all of his life and all of his yesterdays, is he ready to go forward into forever, because then there is no longer the pain of regret or the desire to look back. Then you have fully experienced and embraced the whole of this life here, and you have the wisdom of it locked in your soul.

It is true that there have been many landings of these entities, and there will continue to be. If contemplating them gives you a thrill, that is all right. If, by chance, one lands in your back yard and desires to parlay with you, parlay if you wish; but don't fall on your face and prostrate yourself before them. And don't live for the day that contact might occur, because it may never happen. If it doesn't, what can you say that your life has been for then, eh?

These entities are not planning to take you away. And be glad for that, because what is a paradise to them may be a fright to you. And besides, there are only a few places in the whole of the universe where your biological being, as it is now, could even survive. Before they could take you away on their ships, they would have to pack you in a jelly-like substance just to keep you from falling apart, and most ships are not large enough to have those facilities.

In regard to abductions: These entities know about spirit, God, and foreverness. They possess the knowledge of light and the technology that allows them to be inter-dimensional and inter-stellar. If they possess the knowledge of *these things*, what do they need *you* for? In other words, with all the problems, woes, limited thinking, and bigotry in your life, why would they want you to pollute theirs?

Since they know about all of these things, why have they abducted and examined some of you? Because they haven't been you. Mankind is a mystery to them because they have never lived as one of your species. They desire to understand how your biological and physiological systems work, so they search for answers. You must admit that you are a peculiar group. It is a puzzlement to any *great* mind to understand why *yours* isn't working! That is why they don't sit in their starships and try to channel one of *you*. That is not a put-down, only the truth.

These entities have made contact with many of you, and they have examined some of you to learn about you. And if they wanted to destroy you and your world, they could have done so long ago; they're that powerful. But they are also that loving, for they exist in Superconsciousness.

These entities have been here before in large numbers, and they have taught your ancient civilizations. Do you know why they have not come to teach *this* great civilization? Because this great one just isn't so great. I shudder to think what limited man would do with the understanding of more advanced technology. With *your* pettiness of mind and *their* technology, your solar system would quickly become only a large rim of dust.

Why have entities from other star systems returned to your plane throughout your history? Because they are on a great sojourn, a grand adventure. Forever is a big place, and they stop back here every now and then to say hello and to see what you've been doing for, say, the last 10,000 years or so. It's like going back to the zoo and seeing the new selection of species. Get it?

Master: Yes. Ramtha, do you think it will be possible to visit the inner earth after we've learned to survive and have come out of social consciousness?

Ramtha: Master, what you are going to live through is not going to reward you with visits to alien civilizations. What will become of the human race in the times that are coming will be the beginning of a race of entities who will be more liken unto your brothers in these ships that you contemplate. Mankind will be a race of entities who are without bigotry, prejudice, and limitation. It will be a brotherhood of meek and loving entities who shall, indeed, inherit this plane, for only those of such consciousness will choose to live here. Entities who are still needing to experience pain and suffering, bitterness and hatred and war, will have none here to gratify that need; thus they will choose to exist in other places.

If you desire to be a part of Superconsciousness on this plane, begin the adventure of knowing the most alien entity of all—you—because that is what you must do to see the days to come. Understand?

Master: Yes. Thank you.

Ramtha: If you do that, I assure you, master, you are going to see some most *remarkable* things in your lifetime. Your UFOs shall only be a very small and inconsequential part of them. So be it.

***

24

Being God

What is it to be God? To live as God and to be as God is, is simply to be as you are and to live as you do. Being God does not mean you have to be anything other than what you are, for what you are behind your masks is sublime beauty, awesome power, and the reason for all life. To be as God and to live as God, all you have to do is *be yourself* and live only for your own happiness and joy. You will still retain your unique beauty, character, and style. The only difference is, you are now recognizing that the great and wonderful mystery called God is you in every moment that you breathe, that you live, that you interact with this wondrous plane of existence.

What greater compliment can you give to your beauteous self than to say, "I am this very moment that which glorifies and exalts this moment, for I am that which has created and seen all things as vivid life unfolding before me. I am God, the creator who *recognizes* creation, and without me, nothing exists."

To be as God is to love no thing more than you, to hold no thing greater than you, and to see no thing as more divine than you. To be as God is to allow yourself to think any thought in the kingdom of God and to live in the emotion of that thought.

To realize your godhood is not at all an arduous thing to do. It is simply breaking away from old habits and formulating new ones. It is getting into the habit of calling yourself unlimited god rather than vulnerable man. It is getting into the habit of knowing rather than believing. It is getting into the

189

habit of laughing instead of worrying. It is getting into the habit of seeing the purposeful good in all things instead of finding fault in them. It is getting into the habit of allowing your life to unfold rather than struggling with it.

Learn to be an entity of great humility when it comes to you. The more you humble yourself, surrender to the love of self, and allow yourself to bloom, the greater the glory of the kingdom of heaven will become prevalent before you. Joy is the magic that allows this to occur.

Be kind to yourself and cease comparing yourself with others. Trust yourself and know the virtue that you are. Those things you have unceasingly judged yourself for, *embrace* them, and release them, and allow yourself to be *happy*. When you do, you make room for joy to be realized within you.

Allow self to come forward and be lived. When you do, you will be totally amazed to find that you truly are an entity of great compassion and love. And the virtues you have thought only others possessed, you will find that you possess also.

When you see in yourself the beauty and glory I see in you, you will be able to look into the eyes of all entities and see within them your own reflection, because you now understand that the Father who lives within you, lives within all mankind. When God is realized in self, God is seen in *all* people, all life. Then you will realize that your supreme power and joy lie in the attitudes of compassion and unconditional love. Then you will allow the whole of humanity the same freedom to be and live as the Father within you has allowed your own divine self. For you now know that all entities are neither damned nor lost, but that they are indeed becoming the Father within, *for it is in their heritage to become that*!

Now, the understandings that you are living this moment, and the light you are exuding this moment, will carry you into a grander understanding and greater existence, one that we have been preparing for a long time to allow the beauty of mankind to exhibit a more unlimited mode of thinking. We have prepared a spectrum of life and a new existence that will allow the flesh to live a great deal longer than it has ever lived. And you, who are loved through and through by our beings, are going to know what it is to live as gods in utopia.

Take heart in what you are learning, and take pleasure in your moments of becoming who you are. They are preparing you for a greater day, one for which the majority of you are going to have the eyes to see and the hands to feel and the ears to hear what is going to take place here on Terra, the emerald of this universe.

However long the days that we are together, let them be enriched with new knowledge and the joy that will come from experiencing it. I assure you, what you are learning will reach far beyond even your children's children's children; it will be a way of life for them. And be glad for that, for they are the means for your return to this plane.

You are greatly loved and remembered in all earnestness for everything you do and all that you are. Does the wind know every leaf upon a tree? Indeed it does, for it quivers all of them in its wake.

It is time you begin to believe you are worth something, after all. And when these words need no longer be caught up in the wind and carried to the far reaches of your world, you will see what all of the preparation and all of the fuss was about.

***

25

The Little Gods

Ramtha: (To a four-year-old boy) Lord, will you do me the honor of sitting with me? *(The boy comes up and sits on Ramtha's lap.)* You are beautiful! Are you what is called "a little boy"?

Child: Yes.

Ramtha: Little means you are not grown up, eh? *(The boy nods.)* I will tell you a story, little boy:

Once there was greatness in the sky—thunder in the sky, and lightning in the sky, and a wind that blew a warm rain over a land that was as beautiful as you. And when the gentle wind blew the warm rain over the land called Terra, it nourished all the little things therein, and all the elements rejoiced.

That which created the thunder, and the lightning, and the gentle wind, and the warm rain, were gods littler than you. And the wondrous thing about what they created is that they loved it all! They did not know what is termed evil, or wrong, or ugly, or fear. They knew only love.

When many of the gods came to Terra, and they each became a little child, just like you are, someone told them they were not perfect. And they became scared, and confused, and frightened. That made them grow very tall. It made them grow tall to protect themselves. And they became giants.

When they became giants, one tried to be stronger than the other, more esteemed than the other, more knowing than the other.

The little gods who did not come to Terra looked out the

window, so to speak, and watched with great curiosity as
their brothers, who had grown very tall, became very hateful,
and spiteful, and angry. And they watched them, and they
could not understand. And they began to weep.

Soon, the Father of these little gods came, and he asked
them, "Why weep you?"

And they said, "We know not why they feel the way they
feel; why they cannot feel the way *we* feel."

And the great God, the Father, pondered for a moment, and
said unto them: "Do you still love your brothers who are tall,
who are expressing those things you know not of?"

And the little gods said, "Indeed, we still love them. What
else is there?"

The great God said, "Indeed! What else is there." So he
took the little gods, and he put them in a great force around
Terra, and he called them the Overlords of the Universe. And
the great God said unto them, "You will keep balance in this
universe. And you will be a constant reminder to your brothers, who have grown so tall and have become so limited, of
what purity really is."

Beloved child, there are cities of gods who protect the
entire universe, and they are smaller than you. Yet they can
hold the sun in their hands and the stars upon their fingertips,
and their laughter brings harmony to the world.

I find you most beautiful, because you are like the little
gods who are more powerful, more loving, than the bigger
gods.

Look at your little hand. I have made it magical. When you
feel bad, put your hand upon your being, and it will be well.
When someone else feels bad, put your hand upon them, and
they will be well. When you forget that you are wonderful,
and beautiful, and perfect, look into your hand; it will remind
you of it. And when you think you are small, and helpless,
and powerless, look into your hand. It will remind you of the
little gods who protect all the others, and how small but powerful they are.

(Looks up at the audience) Look at all of them. For them to become what they are desiring to become, they must learn to think as you think.

Never be in a hurry to grow up. Continue to be the magnificent god that you are, just as you are. Be happy with who you are, and be a little child for a long, long time. For all of those who have grown up and have become weary in their lives, are needing to become just like you.

All of them were born knowing gods, just like you were, yet they were brought up to have it reasoned out of them. I will teach them how to be like a little child again.

***

Resources

For Further Study
Of Ramtha's Teachings

Ramtha's powerful, moving, and engaging teachings have had a profound impact on the lives of thousands of individuals since he first began teaching through JZ Knight in 1978. Several of these individuals, out of their love for Ramtha and mankind, have been inspired to share the teachings through written, pictorial, audio, and video formats. For individuals wishing to further investigate and study the teachings of Ramtha, the resources listed below are highly recommended. Books, audio and video tapes are normally available through your local bookstore, or may be ordered directly from Sovereignty. Sovereignty distributes additional books, audio and video tapes of, or relating to, Ramtha's teachings. For a complete listing, write to Sovereignty.

RAMTHA. Edited by Steven Lee Weinberg, Ph.D., this impeccably edited and beautifully designed book presents the cornerstones of Ramtha's teachings. Called by Ramtha "The Great White Book," more than 80,000 copies have been sold since it was published in March, 1986. *Sovereignty.*

Highest quality hardcover $19.95
Special leatherbound edition $29.95

A State of Mind, My Story: Ramtha, the Adventure Begins. By JZ Knight. This is the first volume of her autobiography in which she engagingly recounts her life and her involvement with Ramtha. A love story in the deepest sense of the word. Published October, 1987. *Warner Books.*

Hardcover $8.95
Paper $4.95

I Am Ramtha. A stunning full-color photo essay of Ramtha and JZ Knight, with accompanying teachings. Published May, 1986. *Beyond Words.*

Quality hardcover $24.95

Ramtha Intensive: Soulmates. The first volume of Sovereignty's Intensive Series, this book is an edited transcription of the audience presented by Ramtha on January 10-12, 1986. It is a passionate teaching on the science of soulmates, the degradation of male-female relationships that has kept you and your soulmate apart, and how you can reunite with your soulmate through the power of love. Published September, 1987. *Sovereignty.*

Quality paperback $10

Ramtha Intensive: Change, The Days To Come. The second volume of the Intensive Series, this book is an edited transcript of the controversial teaching presented on May 17-18, 1986. It is an uncompromising look at what man has done to the environment, and what Nature is doing to renew itself. Contains exciting and informative supplementary material edited from more recent audiences. Published September, 1987. *Sovereignty.*

Quality paperback $10

Ramtha and His Teachings. An introduction to Ramtha's teachings in a video format, this tape is composed of excerpts from six video tape sets. An excellent sampling of Ramtha's teachings, character, and teaching style. *Ramtha Dialogues.*

1 Video tape $48

Audience with Ramtha. The most popular video of a live audience, this is a warm, intimate, and colorful presentation of Ramtha's teachings on relationships, passion, living happily, drugs, the science of thought, and many other topics. Also included is a rare interview with JZ Knight. Edited from the audience presented in Honolulu on July 14-15, 1984. *Indeed Productions.*

2 Video tapes $90.00

Love of Self. An audio tape on loving yourself, composed of teachings excerpted from several different audiences. A valuable audio experience on a topic that is central to Ramtha's teachings. *Ramtha Dialogues.*

1 Audio tape $8

Voyage to the New World. Written by Douglas James Mahr, this book is a collection of Ramtha's teachings, commentaries on the teachings and the phenomenon of channeling, and interviews with JZ Knight and other individuals who have grown through their association with Ramtha. Published 1985. *Masterworks.*

Quality paperback $5.95

Manifesting: A Master's Manual. An edited transcript of the November, 1986 Intensive on The Power to Manifest. Simple, direct, and to the point, this very readable book shows how anyone can tap his or her own power of manifestion. *Adams Publishing*.

Quality paperback $7.95

Audiences with Ramtha: Individuals wishing to experience Ramtha in person through attendance at an Intensive or retreat should contact Ramtha Dialogues, PO Box 1210, Yelm, WA 98597. 206-458-5201.

Note: Audio tapes are normally 90 minutes in length. Video tapes are approximately 2 hours in length. Please specify Beta or VHS when ordering video tapes.

TO PLACE YOUR ORDER CALL TOLL FREE
1-800-654-1407
Washington and Alaska call collect 206-376-2177
Visa and MasterCard accepted
10% Discount on Orders over $100

Shipping and Handling: $2.75 for first book, audio or video. $1 for each additional book or video; $.25 for each additional audio. (A video set is considered one video.) Foreign orders, please call or write for rates. All orders shipped UPS unless First Class Mail is requested.

Sales Tax: Washington state residents, add 7.5% sales tax to total.

Money Back Guarantee: The full price of any book or tape (less shipping charges) will be immediately refunded to you if you are not completely satisfied with your purchase. Items must be returned in resalable condition within 30 days of our shipping date.

Note: Prices and charges are subject to change without notice.

Sovereignty, Box 926, Eastsound, WA 98245

BF1301 .R2344 1988   CU-Main

Ramtha, the enlight/Ramtha : an introduction / edi

3 9371 00008 8831

"To Life!

BF 1301 .R2344 1988
Ramtha,
Ramtha

DATE DUE			
APR 22			
NOV 04 '96			

CONCORDIA COLLEGE LIBRARY
2811 NE Holman St.
Portland, OR 97211